The Soulmate Checklist
by Rani St. Pucchi

© Copyright 2016 Rani St. Pucchi

ISBN 978-0-9976977-4-2

All rights reserved. No part of this publication may be reproduced, stored in a retrieval system, or transmitted in any form or by any means—electronic, mechanical, photocopy, recording, or any other—except for brief quotations in printed reviews, without the prior written permission of the author.

Book interior designed by Rani St. Pucchi

Published by

St. Pucchi

P.O. Box 27254
Los Angeles, CA 90027
www.stpucchi.com

The SOULMATE CHECKLIST

KEYS TO FINDING YOUR **PERFECT PARTNER**

Rani ST. PUCCHI

"It happens all the time in heaven,
And some day
It will begin to happen
Again on earth—
That men and women who are married,
And men and men who are
Lovers,
And women and women
Who give each other
Light,
Often will get down on their knees
And while so tenderly
Holding their lover's hand,
With tears in their eyes,
Will sincerely speak, saying,
'My dear,
How can I be more loving to you?
How can I be more
Kind?'"

Hafiz, fourteenth-century Sufi poet

DEDICATION

I dedicate this to all soul mate seekers who have given me encouragement and influenced me to write this book. I thank you and honor you. It is my fervent wish that this will lift and empower all, so together we may add to the beauty of this world and be the beacon for those who seek true love.

Most of all, I thank the late Sufi poet, Rumi, for his inspiration. Without his poetry, this heart would still be grieving.

Sat Nam

CONTENTS

FOREWORD VIII
INTRODUCTION XI
PROLOGUE: IS HE YOUR SOUL MATE? XIX

PART I: GETTING READY FOR YOUR SOUL MATE 1

  Chapter 1: Let's Give Them Something to
             Talk About 4

  Chapter 2: Are You Single and Blissfully
             Happy? Really? 12

  Chapter 3: "Breaking Up Is Hard to Do" 22

  Chapter 4: Are You Ready to Commit? 28

  Chapter 5: Intentional Love: Nine Steps to
             Manifesting Your Soul Mate 36

PART II: MEETING YOUR SOUL MATE 47

  Chapter 6: Is He a Keeper? 50

  Chapter 7: No Sex Without Commitment! 64

  Chapter 8: Trust Your Intuition 72

  Chapter 9: Love and Relationships in the
             Digital Age 80

  Chapter 10: Getting Beyond the
              "In Love" Phase 86

  Chapter 11: Is He "The One"? 96

PART III: LEARNING THE SOUL MATE LANGUAGE....101

    Chapter 12: How Well Do You Know Your Partner? 104

    Chapter 13: What Do You Bring to the Relationship? 114

    Chapter 14: What Do Women Want (in Their Men)? 124

    Chapter 15: What Makes a Woman Irresistible to a Man? 138

    Chapter 16: Twenty-Six Traits that Push Men Away and How to Avoid Them 146

PART IV: GETTING TO "I DO" 163

    Chapter 17: Is He Husband Material? 166

    Chapter 18: Ask Those Questions Now! 180

    Chapter 19: Never Take Each Other for Granted 198

    Chapter 20: Twelve Things Never to Settle for in a Relationship 210

    Chapter 21: Nineteen Relationship Myths: Expectations vs. Reality 222

FINAL THOUGHTS 232
ABOUT THE AUTHOR................................235
ALSO BY RANI....................................238

FOREWORD

MORE THAN 30 YEARS ago, Rani St. Pucchi did the seemingly impossible when she made a name for herself in the bridal gown design industry despite having no formal training in fashion. Her wedding gown designs have been embraced by an all-star roster of celebrities, actresses, athletes, and singers. While that is quite an accomplishment, Rani's range is just as impressive outside wedding couture, where she is making a name for herself as an expert on relationships and female empowerment.

Clearly, Rani was quietly doing a whole lot more than designing gowns throughout her career. She was also listening to brides-to-be as they told stories of finding their soul mates and shared with her their hopes and doubts. The wisdom she gained from these personal encounters as well as her own life experiences are in this new book, *The Soul Mate Checklist*, written for any woman who is dating, afraid to date, or unsure of her partner's commitment or whether or not she has finally found a keeper.

I had the privilege of meeting Rani recently and was so impressed by her mission that I quickly agreed to write the foreword for her new book. As the author of *Chicken Soup for the Soul, The Success Principles* and many other New York Times bestselling books, like Rani, I too believe that the Law of Attraction can be applied to finding a soul mate, and that before any of us can find the love we deserve and that is our birthright, we must first fall in love with ourselves.

In fact, I totally agree with her when she writes, "The relationship you are looking to attract has nothing to do with the other person, but everything to do with you and how you treat yourself."

Amen.

In *The Soul Mate Checklist,* you'll find the blueprint for coming to terms with your past, experiencing unconditional love, avoiding misconceptions about love, and learning what a soul mate is—and isn't. Rani has also included several handy checklists, including one that helps you judge if you have found the "right one" and helps you cut your losses if the guy you are seeing is likely to be unable to commit.

Rani points out that all of us have a soul mate and some of us have more than one. There are people who come into our lives for a period of time, leaving behind lessons that we must learn in order to move forward. This is growth, not failure.

I can't help but wonder what would have happened had my lovely wife, Inga, had a copy of *The Soul Mate Checklist* when we were dating. Guess I'll never know . . . but what I do know is that Rani is spot-on when she writes that it can take more than a few dates before women know whether or not they like a man.

Meanwhile, men everywhere should be grateful that she says women frequently rule a man out too soon. In fact, that could have happened with Inga and me. We met when I hired her to be my personal trainer. She pushed me hard and I didn't like that . . . or her, at first. Somehow we overcame that less-than-promising start, and when we married in the backyard of my home, it was one of the best days of my life.

I hope that after reading The Soul Mate Checklist, you too will find your soul mate to share your life's journey.

—Jack Canfield, Coauthor of the *Chicken Soup for the Soul series* and *The Success Principles*

INTRODUCTION

WHAT IS LOVE?

Not to get too intellectual, let's say love is not just one thing or another. Love is an all-encompassing emotion. The age-old concept includes joy, gratitude, serenity, interest, hope, pride, inspiration, amusement, and awe, among many other feelings. The emotion of love, in its myriad forms, can be one of the most wonderful and uplifting of all feelings.

Most people want love in their lives. The need to feel loved is a primary human emotional need. It is this yearning we feel in our hearts for a beloved. Love is the most desired and talked-about experience, yet it is perhaps the least understood. It transforms the way we see, think, dream, act, and engage in the world. It is also the source of all creative endeavors.

But how do we get to this place to experience true love, the kind that is essential to our emotional health? What is the gift of love we can give another? Ironically, love is both the question and the answer, the lock and the key. It is only by giving what we most desire that we can receive in kind. Discovering that key and opening doors to let in the light is what we yearn for.

Most of us launch into a love affair without really asking ourselves where it will lead. We don't stop to consider that a love affair is only meaningful if we can build something solid from it. We hope that the connection we have with a particular person will last. We fail to ask ourselves if the two of us are in harmony on all four levels—physical, emotional, mental, and spiritual—or whether we are just drawn to the attraction of pleasure and lured by charm.

On the other hand, we often ignore the man who might not give us that big adventurous high; someone we might not even be that physically attracted to but who seems to embrace all the qualities we are looking for. He is responsible; is financially, mentally, and emotionally sound; takes care of himself physically; and is a gentleman. I would say don't give up on this man. Keep dating him, and get to know him better. The drama you had been seeking in the past may not be what sustains true love.

In an age of easy divorces, short attention spans, explosive tempers, low tolerance levels for just about anything, and an unwillingness to compromise or work out differences in the hope of reconciliation, why not step back, take a deep breath, and look long and hard at your future and the commitment you are about to make?

Know that love is not the answer to everything, but it offers us the security blanket that allows us to seek answers to those questions that bother us. Coming from this secure place, we can discuss our differences without condemnation, we can resolve conflicts that may arise, and we can learn to live in harmony in order to bring out the best in each other. Because you are loved, life has a deeper meaning, you feel cared for and nurtured, and you feel free to develop your potential in the secure knowledge of your self-worth. Such is the power of true love.

The need to feel loved is at the heart of all marital commitments, as marriage is designed to meet our soul's longing for intimacy and love. How can we enjoy being with each other and meet each other's needs? How can we ensure that our love tank is always full? These questions sent me on a soulful journey. Along the way, I discovered some powerful insights on how we can recognize our soul mate and what we can do to ensure that we gracefully hold on to this precious opportunity—an opportunity that is offered to us by the Divine.

Having worked with countless brides in my more than thirty years as a designer, and even playing the role of therapist to many, I can vouch for the fact that recovery from lost love is traumatic and does a nasty number on your self-confidence. It can take years to overcome and get back to an emotionally sound and trusting place. With the wisdom gained from my experiences in life and in business, and through the inspired intuition that created this material, I am passionate about teaching you how you can ready yourself and get to a place of attracting and keeping soul mate love, which is the only kind of romantic love that can give you the happiness you long for.

Through my amazingly simple, easy-to-grasp, and practical suggestions, this book will help you make sound decisions, or at the very least, encourage you to take time to understand yourself better before jumping into a commitment. It will guide you to stay open and willing to receive love in its various forms. It will show you how not to expect or demand love but instead check your feelings and intentions, setting them right with pure consciousness, because whatever springs from there will be absolute love.

Throughout these chapters, I take you on a journey to help plant ideas and concepts that will enlighten and empower you to recognize your soul mate when he appears in your life. I believe the knowledge I share has the potential of not only saving numerous marriages but also enhancing the quality and the emotional climate of the relationship you are embarking on.

The principles I share in this book and the checklists I provide you with will work only if you *do* the work and apply them on your journey. They are effective no matter what your current status in life: single and looking for your soul mate; dating or in a committed relationship and wondering if your dating partner is your soul mate; married and wanting to strengthen your bond with your partner and hoping you can be soul mates; or divorced or separated, heartbroken and leery about repeating the same mistakes again, not relishing the idea of going through more heartbreak and more emotional trauma like what you're still reeling from.

This book will be your guide to help you avoid all that. Read it with an open heart and mind so you may gain clarity and recognize the right person when he comes into your life, someone who's a natural fit, rather than trying to *make* yourself fit. Get out of the cycle of dating the same kind of person over and over again just because of the initial excitement he brings to the relationship. Be willing to let go of expectations and recognize the myths that have been holding you back.

Fall in love with yourself first, so that through self-love, you can draw in your loving life partner. Do the inner work necessary to heal your past patterns so that you too can have the "big" love everyone seeks—the eternal, soul mate love. Stay optimistic, and believe. Put your best, warmest, most genuine loving self forward and communicate with kindness and confidence.

It does not matter where you are (or are not) in your relationship right now; the fact that you are reading this book shows you are ready to work toward building a happy life, a lasting relationship, one with your soul mate who is waiting for you even as you are reading these words. The question is, "Are you ready?"

The heart is a funny thing, rarely listening to reason, and most assuredly ignoring any inner promptings that whisper, "Watch out, something is not right here!" So take it easy. Give yourself time in this relationship to know one another before making a lifelong commitment.

Ultimately, you want to spend the rest of your life with someone who you are on "equal grounds" with, where there is a meeting of the mind, heart, and soul; someone you can invite to be with you on your turf and be invited to meet on his so that, together, you can create a life that allows you to be the persons you are meant to be and to support each other on your mutual journey. *That* is the true meaning of a soul mate.

How wonderful it would be if we could glide through life and live from a place of being instead of doing, and make decisions based on our feelings, from our hearts, yet knowing that at the core of our being we are strong, responsible, powerful women who know exactly what we want and are willing to allow the good to come into our lives. Everything in life would just flow. What a fun way to live!

Achieving happiness and finding your soul mate are not just about visualizing and attracting what you want, as many books and programs would have you believe. There are internal blocks you need to be aware of, acknowledge, and remove. There is work that you must do and steps that you must take. Just as a building cannot stand without a proper foundation, you must first have the internal foundation and the mind-set to succeed in love. Once you create the foundation, once you are clear on what it is that you have still to get right, you will automatically be guided to all the appropriate elements that will lead you to overcome what is causing you to live "in lack." The foundation, once secure, will result in your happiness and success. This is what my book aspires to teach you. Ultimately, it is up to you. If you do the work, you will get the results.

There is a vital need for the world's population to understand the underlying cause of personal relationship distress—a belief that there is a separation from each other and ultimately from our true Source. With my guidance, you will gain clarity on the path toward true love, and as a result, overcome fear and stop sabotaging yourself and getting in your own way. The Universe is ready to shower you with love that is far beyond your imagination, once you learn how to receive it.

The book you are about to read was never intended to be a book. The content was written over several years not only as a result of my own experiences, personal tragedies, and traumas—where I was questioning what it was that I was doing, or not doing, and why the things I ran from were the very ones that kept showing up again and again—but also as witnessed in the lives of many others.

The purpose of writing this book is to inspire you and all those who are reaching out for answers to their most pressing questions as to why they cannot find and keep true love. It is my hope that you will benefit from the knowledge I acquired while applying the work in my own life starting almost thirty years ago. My own checklist and techniques allow you to bypass the heartbreaking failures and frustrations of negative beliefs and past conditioning that have kept you stuck. It will elevate your consciousness to become fully aware of what it is that will empower you.

The chapters within each part are not necessarily in an order to be followed sequentially, so you may refer to a particular subject and title for review or reinforcement at any time that suits you. In some instances, I've repeated certain views and words as they pertain to the subject being discussed in various chapters. I believe the repetition will help reinforce their importance and allow your subconscious mind to accept these important principles.

Even though the subject of this book is learning about romantic, soul mate love, you will find that the principles can be easily adapted to other relationships in your life. The information provides the perfect foundation to apply these universal laws and relationship principles for any purpose.

When you apply yourself to the *Checklist*, you will be firmly grounded on your path to abundance, and you will experience the exhilaration of finally achieving the key to manifesting true love. Your shift in thinking will create the fertile soil of the subconscious that will then nurture new ideas of abundance in love of self and of others, allowing an openness to take root so that your success in love can grow. It will inspire and guide you toward the soul mate love you desire.

With this knowledge, and by doing the work on yourself, you will achieve a breakthrough that you initially thought was impossible. Quite simply, the *Checklist* will wake you up and give you clarity and many aha moments that will catapult you to showing up in the world fully present and in your power of knowing exactly who you are and what you are looking for.

The next step is to strengthen your own heart and connect to the vibration of love that you are. Be clear about the relationship you want. Then hand it over to the Divine. You want a divine love relationship, where the two halves are already whole and complete in themselves, and because they have become the best versions of themselves, they attract similar attributes in the other. *Feel* like you already have this soul mate love; put some emotion behind your feeling. *Believe* with every cell of your body that what you ask for is already yours. You know what it would feel like, how happy you would feel. Delve into the happiness and be ready to receive. You are reading this because you are ready to move beyond your present circumstances and fulfill the potential for giving and sharing the deep love that you know in your heart you are capable of. Or perhaps you have met that someone, but you seem to be unable to advance the relationship further. Maybe your soul's deepest longing is for direction, to have your true place in life revealed so that you, too, can find love, the true and long-lasting kind, with a soul mate. Wherever you are on your journey, have faith that romantic, soul mate love is not only possible for you; it is your divine right.

The Universe is alive and loving. As you move toward it, it moves toward you, and you come to glimpse the wonder of life in its infinite forms. Be open to the magic of a love that is beyond your wildest dreams. Welcome a relationship that will allow you to grow the most, to a love of limitless possibilities that is waiting for you.

> "Someone asked once:
> What is Love?
> Be lost in Me, I said.
> You will know love
> when that happens."
>
> —*Rumi*

PROLOGUE

IS HE YOUR SOUL MATE?

> *"It seems we've stood and talked like this before, we looked at each other in the same way then but I can't remember where or when."*
>
> —Lena Horne's "Where or When,"
> from the 1937 musical Babes in Arms

WHAT IF?

What if the soul mate you have been searching for has already come into your life, perhaps several times even?

According to Plato, every human is part of one soul that has been separated. The two halves search tirelessly for one another and do not rest until they come back together as a whole.

We are twinned, but we are divided selves. We have traveled

together from lifetime to lifetime. We've met before, we've interacted with each other before, and we've danced before.

The experience of having known each other for a very long time gives rise to the intense yearning we feel for the other. The beloved is yearning for you as much as you are yearning for your beloved.

Falling in love with a soul mate is a spiritual experience. It's an act of the soul where two souls resonate at the same deep level with the desire for each other. Incredible journeys, personal growth, and professional opportunities take place when this happens, and you feel empowered to execute and accomplish in areas that previously were not possible, all because of the energy each brings to this spiritual partnership.

Suddenly your life takes on more color, more potency, more promise; you feel strength surge through you, and you find yourself living the larger life, taking on new forms together in a conscious partnership. Love then becomes an active creative force in your everyday life.

A soul mate is someone with whom you share unconditional love, someone you can be completely yourself with. You come together in life not only to share a life together but also to grow together as a couple, in good times and in not-so-good times.

Your soul mate inevitably holds not only the aspects of you that are positive, joyous, and wonderful—intense creativity, incredible sensitivity, deep awareness, compassion, and wisdom—but also possesses many of the same aspects as you have that are perhaps not so attractive and loving.

Soul mate love can be rocky at times, but because of the partners' capacity to love deeply, to be intimate, and to connect, they are there for each other to experience the deepest level of healing and to rise above all challenges together in order to accept each other and grow together. And you learn to give each other a little more space to be imperfect.

There is a soul mate for each of us and enough love in the Universe for all. But you have to *decide* if you're ready to create love and be in a soul mate relationship. This kind of deep love and connection is possible for each of us to have, provided we're willing to consciously invest a little time and energy, intention and attention, to attract what we truly want and desire.

Perhaps we have several soul mate relationships in one lifetime. Some soul mate romantic relationships, as with soul mate friendships, come with soul agreements that have an expiration date, and others can last a lifetime. You learn from each other whatever it is you need to learn. As long as you continue to love and grow together, that relationship is enduring.

Sometimes, one person is ready to move on, but the other isn't, and that can hurt. Even so, the relationship will fall away because the contract is over. It's not that there was anything wrong with you, but just that the vibration shifted, and it was time to move on. Rather than seeing your soul mate as being bad, appreciate him as being a tremendous gift to your life for the lessons you have learned and the growth you experienced.

The law of attraction states that we attract to us the people, places, things, experiences, and beliefs that match our vibration and state of being. Therefore, you must send love, be willing, open, and available for love, shift your state of being, your beliefs, and be absolutely clear on who and what you want in your life to draw like a magnet your romantic soul mate and life partner.

Perhaps you have still to meet your romantic soul mate. Although, how do you know if the person you are currently in a relationship with is or is not—or the person you were with before was or was not—your soul mate? Did this person try to show you what it meant to be in a deep, monogamous, trusting relationship? Was it someone who at first you thought was perfect and had everything you ever wanted in a partner? And you rejoiced, knowing how rare a find he was.

Then, as days and weeks turned into months, you realized that he was far from that perfect person you first met, that he, too, had issues with trust and confidence. That he was a little too serious for you, less mature, lacking in qualities that you would have liked, messier perhaps, or less of this and more of that than you had envisioned for yourself.

So you started to have doubts—about him, about yourself, about your future together. You decided that he had to be perfect to be worthy of a soul mate relationship. Because of your own insecurity, you went out of your way to test him, to look for clues and more instances to validate your feelings. You subconsciously tested him by taking actions that would perhaps irritate him:

for example, going out alone with friends and excluding him, spending more time with your family and less with him, just to see how he would react and if he would give up and leave.

After playing games or pushing the envelope at him, you found yourself at a crossroads in the relationship, and it was time to make a decision. Should you leave him, and by doing so, free yourself to meet other men who may be more perfect? Or should you continue to be in the relationship with the man you initially thought was the one for you but now realize falls short of the qualities you perhaps found in other men? How long will you continue to drift from one relationship to another until you find the one you can confidently say is "perfect"?

Or, do you go ahead and settle for this man who, it seems, really loves you and wishes to share his life with you, yet hoping and praying that you can change him after you're married?

You see, in actual fact, many women sabotage their own happiness even when it is staring them in the face. We convince ourselves that he is not a perfect fit after all, and someone else "out there" will be better for us. Confused and shaken, we lose our confidence and fail again and again. We do not allow ourselves to be happy, because somewhere deep inside we believe we are not good enough. Or we convince ourselves we are better than anyone who crosses our path.

Is this not the biggest mistake we make? Looking for love outside ourselves and hoping someone else will complete us? Is that even possible? Can two empty, expectant individuals really make one complete whole? Or do we need to be "whole" inside of ourselves first so that we have something to offer?

If we think of each other at the soul level, then we realize we are all connected. There is really no place where you stop and I start. We are one. But if you think of each other as separate beings, separate bodies, then you create that separation that is not conducive to a true soul mate partnership. This puts us in a perpetual state of hunger, because we fail to recognize it as a spiritual hunger. It's never about what we're not receiving but rather what we're not giving to another in any given moment that is lacking.

A soul mate merely mirrors who we already are. So it stands to reason that if I have a good relationship with myself, then I will attract someone who is equally fulfilled. But first I really need to take a look at how I can show up as the soul mate for the person I am in a relationship with. How can I love from this natural place, share joy and happiness, be compassionate and forgiving to free myself to experience the same?

Inevitably, the failure is in recognizing our soul mate. When we give from our true self—not the ego self—then we automatically recognize and receive love in return. Failing that, the search continues, and we are on a quest to find someone who will fulfill our every need, satisfy our every desire, and reveal to us their perfection.

The truth is that each one of us is made of light and shadow. The question is, whose light is brighter and whose shadow stronger? When we initially meet the one we believe in our hearts is perfect for us, we are attracted to his bright light.

First dates glow, being on their best behavior, making good impressions. Immune to everything else, we only see the bright light he emits, filling us with warmth. As time goes by, we see that, lo and behold, he has a dark side, a shadow, too. It is human nature.

We're not talking dark alley-type shadows, mind you. If there is any hint of domestic violence or a rash, hot temper involving cruelty of any sort, run and run quickly. Rather than casting our light on his shadow and allowing him to light up our shadow in mutual support, we stubbornly insist that we can only settle for the light, and thus reject his shadow.

The choice of continuing the search for a shadowless light is our undoing. Running away from the shadow means we ultimately are turning away from the light that created it. As our space fills with our own light, we suddenly realize the light illuminating the space around us casts a shadow, too. Could it be our own shadow is at times darker and larger than those shadows we've seen and run from in others?

Ask yourself this question: How could it be that this man I am rejecting is able to tolerate *my* dark shadow? How fortunate for me to merge with someone who is willing to cast a light on *my* shadow.

Walking toward the shadow instead of running away from it makes the magic happen. Understanding how our light is enhanced, merging with the other, while easing both shadows in the background is what helps create a healthy, lasting relationship. This is bliss!

Let spiritual love become the bedrock of your life, and you will find that you attract love in everything and everyone, and the Universe will respond to your love by sending you your soul mate. But you are only able to see the love and catch it if you are able to stay open and willing to receive it. A soul mate relationship is your golden opportunity to redefine and recreate yourself.

Envision and visualize your ideal partner; what are the qualities you're looking for in him? Write them down and then work on adopting those qualities in yourself. You don't have to look for the right person; you just have to *be* the right person to call him in. Ask yourself, "How can I *be* that ideal partner?" When you vibrate at that level, you will attract a similar vibrational being to you.

Dwell in that void, which is the eternal realm of infinite possibility. It is God's Will that out of nothing all things emerge. The Universe is intentional. You don't have to *intend* for love to happen. You just have to intend to be a field of possibility that is irresistible to your soul mate to come to you. He is ready and waiting.

The question is: Are *you* ready?

"The minute I heard my first love story,

I started to look for you, not knowing how blind I was.

Lovers don't finally meet somewhere. They're in each other all along."

—Rumi

PART I

Getting Ready for Your Soul Mate

CHAPTER ONE

LET'S GIVE THEM SOMETHING TO TALK ABOUT

LET'S FACE IT. BEING SINGLE IS NOT EASY.

*E*specially when family and friends keep trying to hook you up with men they think are the "right" match for you. They even urge you to get over yourself and settle for a good-enough guy. Your independent female adult life is of great angst and concern to them. The act of tending to yourself, of even daring to exist independently of a spouse and children, is revolutionary and bothersome in their eyes. And what do you do? Out of politeness and consideration, you go along with their blind setups and agree to play nice with their chosen ones for a few hours.

Self-help books and magazines have a knack for informing single women that the reason they are not able to form romantic partnerships is because of their outsized sense of entitlement. Many cultural forces have repeatedly shamed single women for being too picky, petty, and narcissistic.

On the other hand, if you're too busy furthering your career and not investing time in getting out there where you may perchance meet that special someone, then you are missing out. Where do you meet your man? You could start by going where men go, or even delving into the online dating world. In this day and age, you need to invest time to hunt for romance with the same effort and skill as you muster to look for an apartment or a job. Finding the right mate requires your full participation and is worth the effort of your getting out of your comfort zone to seek him out.

The lucky few who have found their ideal partners through blind dates, whether set up by family and friends or through various online dating sites, are few and far between. For most of us, it takes time and commitment and a willingness to be open while trying not to second-guess ourselves.

Invariably, when you have failed to settle for someone so far, your well-meaning friends and family come out of the woodwork with their not-so-subtle hints. Their assumptions that you are unhappy "because of your single status" may not be entirely correct. You are lonely, perhaps, but not desperate.

All sorts of scenarios and comments will cross your path, because in their minds, being single and female equates with unhappiness and inevitably leads to consolation, strategizing, life-coaching, tarot-card reading, tiptoeing, reassurance, and so on. But you know better. He is out there and will be revealed to you when you are ready, or when he is ready, and definitely when you both are ready.

How many of these comments have you heard from well-intentioned people around you? It is an epidemic among older female relatives and married friends wanting to drag you into marrying someone.

1. **"PERHAPS YOU'RE NOT TRYING HARD ENOUGH."**

   What they may not understand is that you're in no hurry and want to take your time to make sure you are compatible with your chosen one. You would rather not rush into a situation you will regret later, especially since marriage to you means "until death do us part." And you certainly don't want to be one of those women who is desperate or feels compelled to marry at the right time rather than marrying the right partner.

2. **"HOW ABOUT DATING ONLINE?"**

   Online dating sites are advertised everywhere, and there is no escaping the onslaught of these ads. It is the world we live in, Internet-fast, with immediate gratification. And, in fact, there have been many success stories of couples that have met through dating sites and have married. Hitting the dot-com sites means being brave and energetic enough to go through a possible series of disappointing encounters and even occasional flat-out rejections. It can sap your optimism and make you raw from the breakups, which are all part of the online game. But "no risk, no gain" is what your well-meaning friends will point out.

3. **"YOU'LL MEET HIM SOON. DON'T WORRY."**

   Of course, no one believes you when you assure them you are not in the least worried about the future! You could actually be enjoying your single and unattached status for the time being. Your work may be your focus at this phase of your life, or perhaps you're enjoying traveling, exploring, and having various experiences. Granted, it would be wonderful to have the comfort, solidarity, and joy of having a loving partner. But if the time is not right, then no matter what you do, how much you're supposed to be worried and made to feel bad, your status is not going to change. You're not closing any doors; you're patient and have faith that your life is not incomplete, nor is it a failure.

4. "ARE YOU SURE HE IS THE ONE?"

"You're damned if you do, and damned if you don't," as the old saying goes. Everyone but you seems to know who is good for you. When you finally meet someone you care enough about to introduce to your parents and friends, they may look at you as if you've gone crazy. Perhaps he is nerdy looking, too tall or too short, not "your type" according to them. Then to put their minds at ease, you sabotage yourself and say you're just "hanging out" together, nothing serious . . .

5. "THE CLOCK IS TICKING."

Anxiety, frustration, and pressure set in if you're constantly being reminded about your age and how if you would love to have kids in your future, the clock's a-ticking. Because fertility has its time frame, if you want children, then you may have to just hurry and consider all your options. How unromantic to have to face the cold reality that you may be in an emergency situation because your eggs are slowly but surely disappearing. Perhaps you could freeze your eggs? So you roll your eyes and say to yourself, "Okay. I'll ask my uterus and let you know."

6. **"HOW ABOUT GETTING OUT MORE OFTEN AND SOCIALIZING?"**

   Attending social gatherings and parties to hunt down a man may not be your thing. Making small talk with people who you don't know well or like very much may be too much of an effort. Then, there is the bar-and-nightclub scene of course, which is also quite intimidating to some. Besides, who wants to marry a man who lives at bars to pick up women? Although you can't judge a book by its cover, because a guy you meet in a bar could be a friend of a friend just hanging out there to humor his friend who's having a bad day, and he's trying to cheer him up and keep him company. If you do attend any of the above, beware of the worst-case scenario: You drop your standards and end up walking out with a creepy guy just because you're supposed to give yourself a chance by playing the field.

7. **"HAVE YOU CONSIDERED GETTING BOTOX/A NOSE JOB/A BOOB JOB?"**

   Beauty is in the eye of the beholder, you tell them. But their suggestions get you thinking. And too much of that (thinking, brooding, pouting) can do a number on your self-confidence. So, you think, maybe. Just maybe. Step away from those thoughts, and if you can, those people.

Having dodged and swerved through the above questions and concerns, you realize pleasing everyone is impossible. On the other hand, ask yourself: Am I being unreasonably picky about whom I will allow into my life? If not, then you are entitled to take your time. Your life can be rich and meaningful, and your bar for your romantic partner may be set high, and that is perfectly fine.

Finding your soul mate and life partner does require some work on your part. If you wanted a really great job, you would not sit back and wait for the job to come to you, now would you? You would be involved in going out there to create it. So it is with wanting to meet your man. You have to take the initiative and make the time, make yourself fully available. If you are doing the work, then I acknowledge you. But if you've convinced yourself that you're too busy and cannot make the time, then it is proof that you really don't have the desire.

On the other hand, if you're stuck in your limiting beliefs, then it may be time to look at them and shift your consciousness. What are you saying to yourself? Do you believe that you are not good enough for someone to love you and that you cannot be authentic to get love? Do you feel you have to sacrifice for love and that you're too much, or not enough, for someone to love you?

The stories that are playing in your subconscious do not serve you. In fact, you are sabotaging your own success at meeting your romantic soul mate because of the energy you are giving out. Just look back on all your past relationships that may not have worked out. You will see that you are the common denominator in all of them, and so there needs to be an adjustment that must now take place to let love in.

Unless we first choose to be a loving person, until we love ourselves enough, we cannot love another. This is what we must work on: to fill ourselves to overflowing and share from that overflow. No one can "complete" you. That is your responsibility and yours alone.

Let's give ourselves permission to love ourselves and recognize true love when it shows up in our lives. In the meantime, you can be happily single and loving your happy, independent life and waiting patiently with conviction, all the while making every attempt on your part to prepare for the quality relationship that you deserve.

> "Forget safety. Live where you fear to live.
>
> Destroy your reputation. Be notorious.
>
> I have tried prudent planning long enough. From now on, I'll be mad."
>
> —*Rumi*

CHAPTER TWO

ARE YOU SINGLE AND BLISSFULLY HAPPY? REALLY?

*S*trange how there is still a stigma around the "single" status even in this day and age.

Do we really need to be in a relationship to be happy? Most of us have no clue as to what makes us truly happy, and so we drift from one relationship to another, looking for someone to fill the void because we're so afraid of being lonely. How about first building a healthy relationship with ourselves? When we feel better about ourselves, we're able to have a more profound and meaningful relationship with someone else.

Almost every woman has had her heart broken at some point in her life. How do we heal a broken heart and allow ourselves to love again? Often, we think we have to rise above the heartbreak and shake it off and go through life as if all is well. The healthy approach is to process our feelings, allow ourselves to mourn, admit how badly we feel, and know that it doesn't necessarily mean that we are not worthy or are lacking in any way.

Obviously, claim responsibility if there is something you don't like about yourself and that you would like to change. Allow yourself to heal, feel the pain, and eventually reach the place where you can honestly ask yourself, "What have I learned from this?"

Look at these failures as stepping-stones leading you to your ultimate relationship—the one with your soul mate. See each person as part of your journey, each teaching you lessons that you have to learn about yourself that will lead you one step closer to the right person, who is waiting for you when you're ready for him.

So often in life, we set goals for ourselves and think that once we achieve them, we'll be happy. We think if we had the right partner; if we had the right job; the new, greatest car; the wonderful, dream house; more money; and so on, we would be complete. Then one day, we realize that we have everything we thought we needed to be happy, to feel good inside, to feel worthy, but we are still not fulfilled. There is that deep feeling in our heart that something is missing. It's that feeling, "I'm not good enough. I need something else. I'm not okay the way I am." There is a void that no amount of things and people can fill. What is still missing, we ask?

SELF-LOVE

Self-love is the key to really getting what you want in life, but getting it in a way that brings deep and true fulfillment. While all the achievements on your list are fabulous, unless you are filled within, unless you're connected to life inside, feeling and full of love inside, you will continue to feel that void. It's your heart that you must nurture and heal. Life can be truly miraculous when you are in the flow—connected with yourself, allowing and receiving all the good that the Universe has to offer.

Ask yourself, "What's my relationship with myself like? How do I talk to myself? How do I treat myself?"

Do you impose conditions on yourself? Such as: "If I did this, then I would be loved"; "If I dressed and behaved this way, I would meet others' approval"?

Our inner dialogue sabotages our own happiness. All the suffering that goes on inside our minds is not reality but just a story that we torture ourselves with. To handle negative beliefs, Byron Katie suggests we ask these four questions:

1. *Is it true?*
2. *Can you absolutely know that it's true?*
3. *How do you react, what happens, when you believe that thought?*
4. *Who would you be without the thought?*

Then turn the thought around to give yourself the opportunity to experience the opposite of what you believe.

Now ask yourself:

1. *What is the most loving thing I can do for myself right now?*
2. *What am I most grateful for about myself and about my life?*

Your inner voice will give you the answers if you will only listen. Give yourself some slack and be generous with yourself; be mindful of your self-talk and change the conversation you have with yourself; take care of what your body and mind need at the moment. These could be simple things that involve pleasure and serve some of your senses—like taking a nap, listening to music you love, taking a walk—activities of pleasure and relaxation that provide balance in your life.

By sending love, ease, and compassion to yourself and to your heart, you release the flow of the chemical oxytocin in your body, also known as the love hormone. This is the hormone that helps us bond and connect with one another, and in this case, to bond with our own heart while sending love to ourselves. We are affirming that we are worthy of love as we feel calm and connected. Look for the good around you and within yourself. Acknowledge what you appreciate about yourself. And savor that.

We jump from relationship to relationship, constantly searching and coming away disappointed. Why not step away from that scene for a brief while and really contemplate? Do you know what you want? Why do you want to be in a relationship? What are you ready to contribute to your partner? What are you bringing into the relationship? All are questions that need to be addressed if you want to stop being on this perpetual merry-go-round and really draw in "the one."

The best way, I believe, to attract "the one" who is going to be the best fit for you, and to gain clarity, is to get blissfully single for a while and to work on becoming complete on your own first. You will attract into your life the kind of partner who is going to reflect how you feel about yourself.

Spend some time investing in falling in love with yourself and recognizing your own inner and outer beauty and the light you have to share with the world. See your self-worth, and by owning all your beauty, you're changing your body's vibration, which will ultimately create a new reality for you. You will see that the only people who show up in your new reality are those who are in harmony with your improved vibration and energy.

Self-love is the basis of a true relationship and the most important aspect to manifesting a soul mate. Unconditional self-love is when you love your whole self, all of you—mistakes, problems, challenges, and every other shortcoming in your eyes. You see these and love yourself anyway. There are no conditions. You believe in yourself enough to be vulnerable and show your true self, and if that person is your soul mate, then he will love you and accept all of you just as you are.

The truth is that a man can't be happy unless you are happy. When you are already happy, he can make you happier. Looking for a person to validate you and make you feel good and feel loved is a recipe for disaster. Knowing this, isn't it time you start to learn to love yourself and learn how to become happy?

If you've been disappointed and hurt and heartbroken from past, failed relationships, you will appreciate that stepping back from the dating scene, no matter how briefly, and being single can help put things in perspective and allow you to regroup and reevaluate what it is that you have done that has not worked and the direction you need to take to avoid the pitfalls.

Start cultivating self-love.

Thinking back on the heartbreaks, which most of us have been through, you know that ultimately you survived. It hurt; it stank; you found yourself wishing you were dead; you curled up in a ball on your sofa for months, perhaps even years, wondering what went wrong. But you survived. You got over it. And in the process, you learned a lot about yourself. And if you will admit it, you even grew as a person. Now, you know why you had to go through all those challenging times. You know that the most important thing you need to do is work on yourself, work on loving and accepting yourself unconditionally. Then you will attract only the people who are vibrating on the same frequency of love as you are. Once you love you, they will love you.

With global divorce rates skyrocketing, more and more of us have found ourselves without partners at some stage or another in our lives. Whether we decide to wallow in loneliness or solitude is totally up to us. It is a personal decision and can be one that tricks and traps us into settling into a comfort zone. But this comfort zone is a mirage because loneliness is destructive, while solitude is productive.

We can make ourselves miserable when we are alone. On the other hand, immersing ourselves in solitary activities, such as getting back into nature, exercising, exploring our surroundings, meeting different people, and being creative will help us know ourselves better and realize our sense of purpose.

We can never be fully aware of our thoughts, feelings, and wants unless we are alone and allow ourselves to think and feel. Being single can be a blessing for those who have struggled to stay in a relationship or have been in one that was not nurturing. It gives us the opportunity to be in a state where we can immerse ourselves deep enough into our own thoughts and minds and feelings that we come out the other side with clarity and conviction about the kind of relationship we want.

Solitude allows us to become more thoughtful, considerate, and content in the long run. When we reach that stage, we become whole and complete in ourselves. We start liking our own company well enough that we will not need to look to someone else to complete us. This is the state of completion you want so that you are not constantly looking for love, or finding love but not keeping it.

Being single allows you to learn to love yourself and ultimately to open yourself to be loved unconditionally by someone else.

For many, single life is just a state they find themselves in between relationships as they sit on the sidelines waiting for the next best thing to happen. Instead of wishing you weren't single, seize this opportunity to take the necessary steps to focus on self-love. Your happiness is influenced by specific habits that you cultivate in your life, so lift yourself up by doing the following:

- ***Spend a few minutes each day in stillness***. Show up for yourself. When was the last time you sat and did absolutely nothing for at least half an hour? Give it a try, even if it feels uncomfortable and perhaps excruciating. You may be overcome with anxiety, and memories of your past relationships may come flooding in. Be present with these emotions and just breathe. Acknowledge your feelings and give yourself permission to *feel*.

- ***Connect with Source, God, Creative Intelligence***. Spend some time praying and having conversations with the Higher Power. When you are in a place of receptivity, you open up, allowing the Divine to enter, and miracles become possible.

- ***Get enough rest***. Sleep well, exercise, and take supplements that contribute to a healthy body and mind. When you are healthy in body and mind, you are able to raise your love vibration and your happiness level so that you become attractive and magnetic to love.

- ***Be grateful***. Think thoughts that support your happiness. Extend loving kindness and generosity toward yourself. Stay in a constant state of gratitude and practice forgiving yourself and others.

- ***Celebrate yourself***. Ask yourself every morning: "What one thing can I appreciate about myself today?" It can be something as simple as your eyes, your lips, your hands, your outfit: When you celebrate yourself, you're changing your entire vibration in that moment by changing how you feel about yourself.

- ***Dwell on thoughts that support your happiness***. Be mindful to process and eliminate thoughts that do not serve you on your journey to self-love, and steer your focus back to happy and peaceful thoughts.

- ***Get out and be among people***. While an inclination to isolate yourself is a common feeling, that will only make you feel lonely. Seeking connection is healthier. Surround yourself with people who support you and your happiness, and create boundaries around the toxic people in your life. Go out with a friend or to a movie, sit at a coffee shop and read, take dance lessons, go to museums, join "meet-up" groups where you can socialize with members who share common interests. This is your chance to practice and perfect your communication and listening skills. It will take your mind off negative thoughts and keep you occupied and interested in the outside world.

- ***Treat yourself well.*** Practice self-care; nurture yourself and do what makes you come alive and feel appreciated. These can include spa treatments, giving yourself gifts and flowers, or taking nature walks or hikes. Doing anything that will help enhance your self-esteem, contribute to a healthy self-image, and increase self-love is worth your time and attention.

- ***Give of yourself to others.*** Get involved with volunteer causes of interest to you. Surround yourself with like-minded people and those who share similar values and interests. It is deeply fulfilling to feel needed and to know that you are making a difference in the world. Get out of your own head and focus on what you can contribute to others. It is the best cure for loneliness and will reinforce your self-worth.

- **Spread the love.** Every day, make it a point to smile and compliment at least five people you meet. These can be passersby on your walk, people you meet when standing in line at the grocery store, at Starbucks, and so on. You will be surprised at how wonderful it will make you feel. You get what you give. That love you sent out will come back to fill your being.

Just as water seeks its own level, your vibrations attract like vibrations. If you want to have an amazing, loving, happy partner, then you must be the amazing, loving, happy person first.

Stop making excuses about why you cannot be happy; stop showing up as a victim in your life and blaming your state of mind and affairs on your parents, your job, your circumstances, or your past. Start taking responsibility by changing your habits now so that you can be content and at peace and love yourself without conditions. Regain your inner confidence by treating yourself as if you matter, by doing things that make you feel loved on the inside.

You may not reach a state of 100 percent loving yourself, but know that the journey, once started, can lead to breakthroughs beyond your comprehension. It's a work in progress. You don't have to be perfect to manifest your soul mate, but by being as loving of yourself as possible and less critical, your effort and your consciousness will make you a happier person. By being open and loving yourself enough to go after your desire to manifest your soul mate, you will bring into your life a person who will support you on your journey. He will reflect how much he loves you, so that in that partnership, you will continue to heal and grow to love yourself more and more.

It doesn't matter how long you've been single and why your past relationships were not successful. Your history does not determine your destiny, so don't allow your old patterns to hold you back or interfere with your ability to have love now. Don't shut down your heart to having love in your life. Stay open and believe. Learn from your failed relationships and ask yourself, "What do I need to learn from this? How do I want to love myself so that others can love me the same way?" The truth is that if you truly desire and have that deep longing in your heart for love, it will be possible and available for you.

Love your life, and for now just focus on creating the best relationship you can with yourself. Instead of looking externally for what you want out of life and love, do what is necessary to create the shift to change negative patterns and release your past challenges. Make a pact with yourself that you will take a stronger look at the things that have not served you and you have no control over, and make positive changes beginning today.

In the meantime, enjoy your single life and live in the moment. This is your chance to focus on you and let go of the past and heal yourself. Rest assured that you are not alone and that there are other people in a similar situation as you who would be delighted to connect with you. Have faith that when you believe how special you are, you will meet that special someone you have been waiting for. And that, my dear ones, is bliss!

> "Keep knocking, and the joy inside will eventually open a window and look out to see who's there."
>
> —Rumi

CHAPTER THREE

"BREAKING UP IS HARD TO DO"

The title of this chapter, a song by Neil Sedaka released in 1962, pretty much sums up how one feels when a relationship ends. It's a phrase that has been uttered by countless people who have experienced heartbreak and struggled to recover from broken relationships.

Failed relationships and heartbreak can take a toll on our psyche. Sometimes the heartbreak endures not months, but years, and you wake up one morning to the realization that the world has moved on but you are still stuck in the same place. You can't seem to be able to get over that someone, even though it may have been you who did the walking.

You're not only mourning the death of the relationship but also having this continuous dialogue inside your head on what went wrong, how you could have done things differently, and how it could have worked. Or perhaps you are convinced something is wrong with you. You start having a pity party, except this party has been going on for a long while, and even those near and dear to you have taken their leave.

What is the mourning period allowed when one experiences loss? Experts say six months, a year at the most. But what do they know? They have not walked in your shoes.

I believe that the main reason why people can't let go and move forward has much to do with their past. When they suffered previous losses growing up, or when they suffered rejection or neglect, their needs weren't attended to. Later, as adults, they are still searching for love but haven't learned how to have a healthy relationship. They can't let go of the past because they're still not done dealing with those previous losses.

Deep down, men and women often believe there is something unlovable about them, and they are afraid they will never meet someone else who will love them. So they hold on for dear life to whatever form of love they can get, even if it means being in a relationship that is abusive or unfulfilling.

The only way you can correct and heal a broken heart is when you are ready to accept, acknowledge, and release. No one else holds the key to your well-being, nor do you need anyone else's input, presence, or permission.

Here's some work you can do on your journey to healing and wholeness:

1. **RECONCILE YOUR PAST.**

    What was it that you needed but did not get growing up? Was it something that you had wanted but failed to ask for, or perhaps it was something that had happened that you knew was not right but chose to ignore? Become aware of the heart of your hurt.

2. **MAKE A NEW CHOICE.**

    Choose to love yourself more. Tell yourself that staying hurt or angry does not serve you but is, in fact, robbing you of a beautiful life that is waiting for you. Convince yourself that making yourself right and someone else wrong does not make you more loving.

3. **CEASE CONTACT.**

   Until you have gotten yourself to a happier place, until you have overcome your hurt and anger and reached a place of higher self-esteem, cease all communication with the person in your old relationship. Resuming contact may not happen until far into the future, or perhaps it may never happen, but so be it.

4. **REMEMBER THE BAD.**

   This may be counterintuitive, but if you can't get over your loss, it is probably because you're still idealizing the person and have forgotten all the bad stuff that happened in the relationship. The thing to do is to write down daily at least three to five hurtful things that your ex said and did to you and read them. Use this technique until you have convinced yourself and believe that it really is best for you to move on.

5. **LET IT GO.**

   Now that you've done steps one through four, you're ready to let go. Start getting clear about the person you want to be and the type of relationships you want to attract into your life. Then ready yourself to show up in the world in a different way.

6. **CULTIVATE SELF-LOVE.**

   Your relationships are like a mirror reflecting yourself back to you. The kind of love you draw into your life is dependent on the kind of love you extend to yourself. Take care of you, and fill yourself with love and self-esteem. You will attract the vibration that is in sync with your own vibrating energy.

7. **VISUALIZE.**

   Be clear on what you want in your next relationship. Spend time visualizing what characteristics you would like your next partner to embody: his sense of humor, his way of expressing love and affection to you, your shared values, your future goals together, experiences you would like to have together, and so on. When you start visualizing your future, the past failures recede into the background, and you will find yourself thinking less and less about your ex.

Are you committed to moving forward in life? Have you given yourself permission to leave the past behind? It is your choice. Remember to give yourself time to clear the emotional issues before jumping into a new relationship. Course correct when you find yourself falling back, and above all, do be gentle with yourself.

Time heals all wounds.

"Today, like every other day, we wake up empty and frightened.

Don't open the door to the study and begin reading.

Take down a musical instrument. Let the beauty we love be what we do.

There are hundreds of ways to kneel and kiss the ground."

—Rumi

CHAPTER FOUR

ARE YOU READY TO COMMIT?

*I*t was a beautiful October Sunday. I was taking my morning walk in Griffith Park, enjoying the shadiness of the green trees and admiring all the different kinds of flowers that were in full bloom.

I hiked over the bridge and ran into my neighbor Laura. A brilliant, successful business owner, Laura is one of those Type A workaholics, extremely decisive and smart. However, in the relationship department, she seemed somewhat challenged. In the years we have known each other, we've become quite close, and I have met at least half a dozen men she's dated: handsome, warm and caring gentlemen, generous to a fault, and extremely successful in their careers. I have seen the love and affection they have showered her with; many have even proposed marriage only to be turned down.

Today, she came up to me, and as we were talking, she asked me one of the most profound questions I've ever heard: "Rani, how do you know when you are ready to commit?" I knew why she posed the question. I've seen Laura struggle in and out of relationships, ending them before they even had the chance of blossoming. She never thought she was ready, always waiting for a perfect man to show up. Laura was at a crossroads and wondering whether she was finally ready to commit.

So many supertalented, successful women who believe they are open and ready and willing to manifest love are having such a hard time. They have created a successful life in one area, but when it comes to love and relationships, they're frustrated and lost. They are strong, successful, and powerful, with the utmost confidence in every other area of their lives—except in love. They feel that just as they do in their businesses, they have to *drive* themselves for love, not realizing that what they really need is to get to a place where they must *nurture* themselves for love.

They must start asking the bigger question: "What does my soul want?"

They seem to be in this vicious cycle of weaving in and out of relationships. They read and talk about relationships, they go to seminars to learn about relationships, but even so, they are clueless on what to do to move their relationships forward. They are stuck and go through the motions of dating but never committing, almost as if they are waiting for permission from others, not trusting their own instincts and judgment.

The question "Are you ready to commit?" seems simple enough. But the answer may perplex us all. For how can we be absolutely certain that we are ready to commit to a long-term relationship, especially marriage?

THE STEPS TO COMMITMENT

The first step is to **gain clarity**. Get quiet to gain clarity on what your soul is most calling for. When you're so busy working and being in the world, you're in drive mode, constantly doing, doing, doing. Taking a step back and really getting into a place of loving and nurturing yourself is very important to gaining clarity.

Rather than *wanting* the relationship, passion, and intimacy, make space and go inward; get into a place of quiet contemplation and ask yourself what beliefs you are holding onto. What stories are you telling yourself that are preventing your goodness from coming into your consciousness? What proof are you looking for out in the world to reinforce those stories? By constantly playing mental games with yourself about what you can't have, why you can't have it, and why you shouldn't have it, you're drawing those realities to you.

Sometimes, it can be as simple as changing your mindset, opening up to a different belief, and shifting your focus. Instead of struggling to make something happen, entertain the possibility of something bigger and better showing up, and then be receptive to it. Rather than placing responsibility and blaming outside forces for things not happening, look inside with compassion and love and stop rejecting yourself.

We teach people how to treat us by the way we treat ourselves. The person you're trying to attract and love cannot come into your life unless you are attracted to your own persona and love yourself. Learn to value yourself first, and know you are worthy of love. The relationship you're looking to attract has nothing to do with the other person, but everything to do with you and how you treat yourself. Be open to changing your beliefs and tap into your inner wisdom—that voice of unconditional love—to receive the love you want in your life. You are the authority of your life, the creator, the only one responsible for your happiness.

Changing our stories about past breakups helps a great deal in propelling us to move forward in life. If you believe that a marriage or relationship somehow "failed," then reframe that story and create a new one around it. Tell yourself that the relationship had run its course and was ready to end anyway. It doesn't mean that it was a failure. It doesn't mean that the person wasn't your soul mate or that the love wasn't real. Look at it like this: You were meant to be together for a while, to go through your journey to complete what you had signed up to do together, and then it was time to move on.

Each one of us has a soul mate; perhaps we will even have several in one lifetime. Some soul mate relationships, as with soul mate friendships, come with an expiration date, and others can last a lifetime. You learn from each other whatever it is you need to learn. As long as you continue to love and grow together, that relationship is true and strong. Oftentimes, the agreement ends when the vibration shifts. Sometimes, one person is ready to move on but the other isn't, and that can hurt. Even so, the relationship will fall away, and the contract is over.

The next step is to know that you truly **desire** a soul mate relationship. When you have that deep desire and clear intention, your soul mate will appear in your life. Just as you have the desire to meet him, he also desires to meet you. What may be causing the delay and getting in the way of manifesting is some ingrained idea, or a false belief, or some unhealed wounds.

If that is the case, then you must **be aware** and vigilant. The delay in meeting your soul mate could even be about lack of visibility, as when you're out in the world but not really paying any attention to your surroundings or who is in your vicinity. Fate might be trying to send you the right person, but your attention is on your smartphone, and you keep missing him when you're in line at Starbucks or at the grocery store. You're texting or you're talking and doing everything except opening your eyes and being aware enough to see who may be looking at you. Those are distractions that you may want to mindfully omit from your life.

And while you're waiting for love to come into your life, you can start to **live "as if."** When you're living from this state, then your behavior matches your belief. Be happy and excited as you go about your day-to-day life, anticipating the physical arrival of your soul mate. Your actions and your behavior are showing the Universe that you know and trust that the one you've asked for is already yours and that you're already part of this amazing partnership.

Make space in your life and create the right atmosphere, the right vibrational frequency in your surroundings. Set a table for two, wear sexy lingerie and make space in your closet and your bedroom. Get your home ready. Get rid of any past mementos, pictures, or keepsakes that bring to mind your past relationships, which can become your love blocks. By taking these steps, you're making space for that someone you will share your life with. Your manifesting power becomes unstoppable, and you're sending clear and strong messages to your subconscious that things are changing, and you're letting the Universe know that you are indeed ready and prepared for your soul mate to enter your life.

The law of attraction states that we attract to us the people, places, things, and experiences that we think and feel about. Believe and feel in every cell of your body that what you've asked for is already yours. Be grateful to the Universe for all the love you share and experience with your soul mate. Feel as if he is already in your life because the feeling component is the secret sauce that will bring about what you most desire. So *feel* with all your being and *believe* that you deserve it. See it not with your head but with your heart. Your feelings and your pictures must match up. Be in a state of love and appreciation and gratitude and present-moment awareness, and above all—trust.

If you're fully committed to making your love life your priority, then you have to shift your attention and make time in your busy schedule to actively pursue your dreams and pour your creative energy into the process. Relationships take time. Dating takes time. It's not enough just to take all the other steps to manifest. Take time also for self-love and self-care; take the time to spend online if you're seeking to meet people on dating sites. These things can be life-altering, but you must do the work. Be intentional and take action while simultaneously surrendering and detaching from the outcome.

RELEASE AND LET GO

Things don't happen on the timeline you set. Know that divine timing is perfect because the one you've been asking for may not be ready yet. Know that he is worth waiting for. Your job is to stay the course, take action, be open, and trust; be willing, ready, and available.

If you're trying to change your world without changing yourself first then the result of getting knocked back can throw you off course completely. If your inner foundation is not solid, you are not able to continue forward because you have not developed solid bedrock to fall back on.

What is your inner self-talk? If you're still hanging onto certain love blocks, feeling unworthy, telling yourself things such as "I'm too fat," "I'm too old," "I'm too broke," "I'm too damaged," "I'm unlovable," "I'm not successful enough," or even worse, "I'm too successful," this would be a good time to get over all these sabotaging beliefs. They do not serve you.

What are your core beliefs? Are you a woman who values herself for what she can *do* and what she can *accomplish* rather than who she really *is*? Are you completely focused on what you do and create? Have power and achievement taken over your life?

What is your biggest fear about finding love? Many women are afraid of getting into a relationship and investing their time and energy because they think it is ultimately going to end; that he might stop courting her; that he might not like her anymore after a time; that marriage might neutralize their relationship. They are afraid of having to go through the vicious cycle of heartbreak and recovery again and again. Sometimes, you just have to get outside your comfort zone and be willing to fail.

When you are unkind to yourself, it comes out subconsciously in your language and in your conversations with others. People can sense your energy, intention, and internal state. If you are enigmatic and aloof, you can turn people away, and you're clearly not ready to commit.

Have you healed your past heartbreaks, come to terms with your past, done deeper, inner-transformational work on your heart and soul to heal? Are you willing to be in chaos for a little while and let your feelings move through you, process them, and see what happens? You will see things start to shift as you work on yourself and become more open.

You want to be ready for a man who can meet you at the level of consciousness that you are seeking. If you're not over past hurts and are still nursing old wounds, then you shouldn't be seriously pursuing anyone, as you probably still have trust issues.

Is perfectionism holding you back from meeting your soul mate? Many women think they have to be perfect to find love, that they must be a certain size, have their career together, be completely successful, have a nice car and that perfect house, and be completely out of debt before they can find their soul mate.

Alternately, they feel that the man they meet must have *every* positive trait on their list of an ideal partner. You may have this notion that you still have to find that one person who is supposed to be your soul mate, but you don't realize that's not the issue. The issue is that once you've found that one person and you are close to him, you get cold feet.

If you are such a woman, you are sabotaging your chances of finding true love. Can you handle a relationship without imposing unrealistic demands of your "ideal partner"? Can you allow him to be and accept him for who he is?

Ask yourself these profound questions: Is it truly your deepest desire to find your soul mate? Is your heart open to receiving love? Do you find yourself conflicted in your desire, with one foot on the gas and the other foot on the brake? You're not getting where you want to go, because you're afraid or unconvinced that it is possible for you.

Are you ready to be vulnerable and show up so emotionally naked that you can completely share all of you and go to an intimate personal place that such a union calls for? Vulnerability is not weakness. On the contrary: It takes a brave person to be vulnerable; to risk showing your most private self takes courage. When you come from this place, your partner feels inspired to share back, thus allowing for a deeper connection.

> "There is a path from me to you that I am constantly looking for, So I try to keep clear and still as water does with the moon."
>
> —Rumi

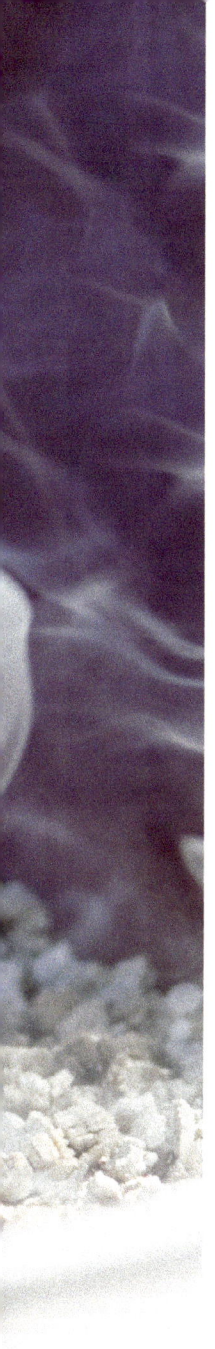

CHAPTER FIVE

INTENTIONAL LOVE: NINE STEPS TO MANIFESTING YOUR SOUL MATE

"Everything in the universe is within you. Ask all from yourself."

—*Rumi*

A bride visited my trunk show in New York and had me design a custom wedding dress for her. I asked what date she would need it by, and she told me that actually she was not even dating anyone.

In fact, she had not gone on a date for three years, focusing on growing her business instead. Now that her business was up and running, she decided to take action steps that would send a clear message to the Universe that she was ready to meet her soul mate and get married.

Six months later when her dress arrived, she hung it in her closet in an obvious place where it would be visible to her every morning before she left for work and every evening when she returned home. She sent it love and visualized her husband being there with her. She had imaginary conversations with him every day. She was convinced that he was on his way.

Within two months of receiving her dress, she met her future husband at a restaurant, and they got engaged a mere thirty days later. She is now happily married.

Now *that* is acting "as if" and being intentional!

WHAT ARE *YOU* DOING TO MANIFEST YOUR SOUL MATE?

Do you feel like you are constantly spinning your wheels on finding true love? You're reading books on love, listening to all the wise gurus talk about love, attending seminars on love, and even being coached on how to find true love. You're looking for, hoping for, even praying for, but not finding, your soul mate.

You've dated enough men and given consistently of your time and emotional energy only to be disappointed. You have yet to meet the kind of partner that you would be happy with, someone with whom you can create a loving, long-lasting relationship. As years go by, you have become more and more disappointed about the opportunities out there, and you have drawn the conclusion that if you are meant to have love, then it will "just happen." And if it hasn't happened yet, then it must mean that you are not meant to be in a relationship. So you've resigned yourself to being alone.

What are you doing to attract true love to you? Perhaps you are afraid of love and are subconsciously sabotaging your chances of finding it without even realizing it?

Have you consciously said to yourself, "I'm ready for a real, big love to share my life with, a beloved, a soul mate"? But having said that, are you *truly* ready to welcome that person into your life? Have you done the inner work, losing your fears and limiting beliefs around love?

Could it be that the types of men you gravitated toward before are part of what you could now call your "old love blueprint"? If so, you need to open yourself to a "new love blueprint," to meet someone who might not even be your "type." Sometimes, our soul mates don't look like what we expect them to look like.

Perhaps you're an overachiever and a perfectionist and have a deal-breaker list a mile long for that someone to live up to before he will even be accepted into your life. And everyone you have met and been with so far has some flaw or other that does not conform to your image of your life partner.

Is it possible that you are hiding your normalcy, and deep down inside you are just like all women—someone who wants to give and receive love? But you're afraid because you believe that if you allowed someone to get too close to you, he could hurt you. How exhausting!

One thing is for sure: Nothing you have done so far has worked. And you will not experience the love you desire in this lifetime unless you consciously do something very different to create a different outcome. Instead of wishing and hoping for love—the lasting kind—thinking that if you want love it will just happen to you, set a clear intention to be a "creator."

Set an intention with all the resources that have been given to you and take a stand to create what you most desire. Devote time and attention to focusing inward to discover, and begin healing unresolved patterns and your need for absolute perfection that is keeping you from making better choices.

Your own inner and outer consciousness and your beliefs in your power to create are at your disposal. In order for love to happen to you, you must make an effort to go toward *seeking*, *allowing*, and finally *receiving* it.

Neither forcing love to happen nor becoming passive about having it will work. You don't have to scheme, to seduce, to plot to make it happen. All you have to do is make a commitment to show up and be a creator of what you most ardently desire. Be *receptive*. Let go of *control* and *allow*. Just *trust*.

You are limitless energy, a powerful creator. You have the power to manifest extraordinary love. The choices you make can foster true joy and love into your life. The energy that you pour into your efforts will create your desired experiences. If you are not living the life of your dreams, it's because on some level, you have created blocks that are keeping you from everything you desire.

Create a vision for love that is bigger than you can imagine. Decide that you're ready to attract that soul mate into your life. Believe. Visualize what it will feel like when you have what you desire. Then show up in ways that are consistent with your vision. This intention and implementation may be out of your comfort zone, and even though you doubt that success is guaranteed, if you don't try, how will you know?

Here are steps you can take now:

1. **STOP TELLING YOURSELF OLD STORIES.**

    Your past and the stories that you tell yourself of why and how you have failed or what someone else did to you do not serve you and are blocking your bright future. Have courage and be willing to let go of the stories that are holding you back from receiving the things you most desire. You may have become jaded, believing in the lack of quality men, ones who are trustworthy and loving, men who are able to meet you where you are in life. Your deep-seated beliefs and the need for absolute perfection covertly disempower and diminish the men who you are with. Decide now that you will not let the past define your future. Leave the past in the past, where it belongs. Surrender the judgment, the blame, the shame, and the guilt for others and for yourself, and move into a space of *choosing*. Choose now to let go of self-condemnation, unkind thoughts, and unworthiness, and open yourself to gratitude and forgiveness. Step into this moment. Go out and make different choices. Become conscious of your thoughts and internal dialogue. They do not belong in the place where you are going now.

2. REMOVE ALL THE BARRIERS YOU HAVE CREATED.

What are you currently doing, or not doing, that is blocking your "good" from coming to you? What are you saying to yourself, about yourself, about others, that is repelling love? Change your story, your core beliefs that may be sabotaging your relationships. And remove all the blocks, which you may have subconsciously created, that are stopping you from receiving what it is that you desire. You are being given a chance to heal, to see your past differently, to make different choices, and to do it over. You want to go into this being your very best self. Be completely you. *A Course in Miracles*, a spiritual guide for life by Helen Schucman, says, "Your task is not to seek for love, but merely to seek and find all the barriers within yourself that you have built against it."

Do the work to make yourself impeccable. Decide you are going to be a success story and then live like one. Become *aware* of the thoughts and barriers you have created, and *accept* yourself exactly as you are now. Then move forward and take *action*.

3. EXPAND YOUR CAPACITY FOR LOVE.

Be the amazing partner you want to attract. Have a healthy self-esteem and expand your beliefs about your worthiness as they relate to how lovable you are. Send "loving kindness" to yourself. Do the inner work and raise your love vibration. If you're not conscious, you're not going to attract a conscious partner. Become the person you wish to meet. Acknowledge yourself for the things that are absolutely amazing about you. Know that you were born to give and receive great love and expand that capacity for love in yourself. Expand your comfort zone by stepping out of your comfort zone. Do things differently. You really don't know how you're going to meet your soul mate. The possibilities for you in the areas of love are endless. Open yourself to those possibilities.

4. **SHOW UP.**

    Put yourself in situations and go to appropriate places where you may meet that special someone. Show up really interested and available. Show up as an ecstatically happy woman as you walk and talk with this new sense of yourself, with the right mind-set of possibility and adventure, of excitement and wonder, from a place of curiosity and exploration and learning. Show up as your authentic self, with confidence and the conviction that you are valuable, wanted, and worthy of the most amazing relationship. There is no one you need to be other than yourself to create love. Let go of control; be authentic and trust that your true love will reveal himself when the time is right.

    Online dating is another way to get out there. If nothing else, it is an opportunity to find out more about who you are, what makes you tick, and what kind of a relationship you are looking for. Show up in a way that is very self-focused and in ways that will create evidence for this being true.

5. **WRITE IT OUT.**

    The power of the written word cannot be underestimated.

    Write your intentions: *My perfect soul mate is on his way to me . . .*
    What are the qualities of your soul mate? List

those qualities and be specific.
What do you most deeply desire to experience?
What do you want or desire in your partner?

Describe how you want to feel and experience in the partnership:

*I want to feel loved and respected.
I want to feel excited about life.
I want to feel appreciated.*

Feel it. How does it feel to be loved?

*What does it feel like to be appreciated, to be respected?
As you do so, you bring that energy and the vibration to you.*

Repeat. Keep repeating the process continuously for the next forty days, and then be open to receiving.

Step into the identity of already being in the relationship, knowing that your partner already loves and adores you and has been searching for you his entire life. By writing it all out, you are activating a *field of synchronicity*. Doorways will open to allow you to walk through to witness the magic that is available. The right messages, pertinent books, and teachers will appear in your life. However, it will be up to you to be present enough to recognize these messages as they pertain to your life at the moment. You are a "creator," and the love that you seek is already yours. Believe it and you will see it.

6. **DISCARD ALL LIMITING BELIEFS.**

There is a virus going around in our society that tells us we must be a certain way, a certain weight, a certain height, a certain age to have love in our lives. Those are all lies. Those "limiting beliefs" do not serve you. Fact is, there is a conscious man out there who is the perfect person for you in the exact place where you are in your life now, someone who is willing to embrace all of you—the authentic you—and love you without any conditions. But you must be open, willing, and available, and make yourself visible to discover him. Believe and it will be so.

7. **AFFIRM.**

   Write down affirmations and read them with conviction daily and often until they seep into your subconscious and become your core beliefs. Affirmations are your power statements and can create a permanent shift in consciousness to create a transformation that is short of miraculous. Affirmations can be as simple as: "I am the creator of the great love I seek"; "I am worthy of receiving love"; "I am an awesome, gifted, creative, talented woman with so much to offer"; "I am perfect and whole just as I am"; "I have the power to attract and create a partnership with someone who meets me on every level"; "I am ready and willing to meet my soul mate now. I accept him in my life now"; "My perfect love is here to stay." Read your affirmations every morning upon waking and every night before going to bed. Feel that it is already so. Breathe it all in.

8. **SET AN INTENTION AND VISION.**

   Start envisioning the committed life partnership that is possible for you.

   Intentionally connect with your desires and envision your future, the kind of love partner and the experiences that you desire. Imagine your partner standing in front of you, with you, until you get a clear sense of who you would need to

be and show up to receive this amazing love in your life. What does this love feel like, what does it sound like, what does it taste like? Having done this, you will have shifted your old identity and gained clarity about what you need to embrace to fully receive love. Then step into having all that you desire.

9. **RAISE YOUR LOVE VIBRATION.**

    Love is not an emotion. It's an energy that is vibrating at a frequency most powerful on this planet. You are a vibrational being. Whatever you focus on activates a corresponding vibration in you. If you're focusing on lack and unfulfillment, desperately thinking that you're unlovable, that you're destined to be alone because there's a shortage of good men out there, then that is the vibration you are emitting. That energy then goes out as a magnet and attracts to you what you really don't want. You are not able to express your feelings, the experiences, needs, and desires that you are yearning for. Your erroneous beliefs need to be corrected by understanding where the emotions are coming from, what they are telling you. Then recognize, embrace, and stay with them as long as you need until you have created a shift in your subconscious.

Once your heart is freed of the blocks to the love that you are, you move into a higher vibration. Conscious choice, gratitude, and forgiveness play a crucial part in your healing and will help raise your love vibration. The joy comes back in, and you find your voice; you can now stand up and bring your light into the world. You are a magnet, and you will attract your perfect partner who is also vibrating at the same energy level as you.

Recognize that this is an intentional process and know that you have the power to create the love you want. You do not need to know how it will happen. All you need is a clear vision and an absolute certainty that what you are looking for is also looking for you.

Be willing to consider having what you want. *Serendipity* and *synchronicity* work in your favor, but you must help the Universe bring what you want to you by being clear and willing to have the relationship with the man of your dreams. Allow yourself to *feel*; be willing to experience what it feels like to want soul mate love, and then imagine having it. Your vibration can be felt.

Make time for love. Take personal responsibility to heal yourself and be completely transparent and clear about who you are and what you want. Be grateful for all your past experiences, good and bad, for they have brought you to this moment.

Know you are truly supported, truly loved, and you have the opportunity and the gift to truly love someone now. Keep doing the work and putting yourself out there. You are a walking magnet. What you put out into your consciousness is going to magnetize whatever comes into your life.

Embody your brilliance. Own your power, speak your truth about yourself and your life, adopt healthy beliefs and behaviors around relationships, and soul mate love will become your destiny.

You are the extraordinary, awesome, brilliant woman who your soul mate is seeking. Awaken to the deeper truth of your very existence and know that you are worthy of love. You can let go of control and show up in the full power and presence of who you are.

Move through the world with openness and presence, receptive and attentive to synchronistic signs. Make choices and take actions in alignment with the future of the love that you seek.

Something magical is coming your way. Just *allow*.

"Your longing for me is my message to you. All your attempts to reach me are in reality my attempts to reach you."

—Rumi

PART II

Meeting Your Soul Mate

CHAPTER SIX

IS HE A KEEPER?

Dating can be an exciting phenomenon. You're having butterflies, you're nervous, and you're excited, and you're wondering: "What's he going to be like?" "What's going to happen?" "What are we going to talk about?" "Will we feel a connection or not?" "What will he think of me?" "Is he going to like me?" "Will he choose me?"

You feel like you can't breathe as these thoughts drift through your mind; all your energy, emotion, and attention is focused on how you should act so he will accept and like you.

Being in this anxious state can cloud your perception. When going out on a date, it's best to take a deep breath, bringing all your energy and focus back to *you*. Be aware of where your energy lies; is it inside or outside of you? Center yourself. Be at peace and trust in yourself. Trust in the Divine.

Be the love you want to attract. Be clear who you want to let in. Ask yourself before going on a date: "What am I feeling?" "What am I focused on?" "How do I want to feel?" Make sure you're not going in with a "feeling of lack" and desperation for love. Change your vibration by going inward and practicing a few minutes of visualization; ask for divine guidance so you can be aware enough to recognize and weed out men who are not right for you. It's also the fastest way to attract the right man to you. You will recognize each other by the energy and the vibrations you both exude.

Finding your soul mate takes time and patience. We are so often disillusioned and disappointed. We feel as if we're running out of options, and every man we date seems to be the wrong man. We feel helpless, hopeless, undesirable, and really, really angry and stupid.

You're probably familiar with this scenario. You've been through the mill with relationships, and you're armed with an ambitious dating plan, only to see it fail every single time. All the while, you've never stopped to ask if the other person is worthy of love or what it is that you are looking for in a life partner.

Then one day, you meet a man who seems genuinely interested in you. He asks how you're doing, about your likes and wants. Soon, you realize he isn't really interested in your personality or what you do, your beliefs, or even who your friends are. All he wants is to have a good time and see how he can get you to have sex with him. This is when you set ground rules and lay down your requirements. You're not looking for a fling.

Have you ever been with a man who for months has treated you as if you're his soul mate, only to withdraw suddenly and leave you hanging? Or you know that things are perfect between the two of you—you've been seeing each other for quite a while now—but it feels like he's stalling, and the relationship is stuck, which causes you to worry that it'll never get moving forward again.

You think you're in love, and you feel chemistry, but the other person doesn't reciprocate. You think something is wrong with you as opposed to questioning if the person you're with has the capacity to love. You do all the things that a wife would do. You support him emotionally, you are loyal, and you tell him and show him how much you love him. You are close to his family, and they seem to be close to and like you, too.

He seems excited when you call him. He plans trips and then he cancels them. He says he will be there at a certain time, but he's always late and doesn't call to let you know, or he cancels at the last minute.

You give and give and love and love, yet you get so little in return. You are beating yourself up for feeling desperate for attention and affection and a commitment that may never be forthcoming. He has still not asked you to marry him, and you start having doubts. Perhaps you're really not the one he wants, or heaven forbid, he is married to someone else and you are not aware of it.

If that is the person you're with, then leave him. Let him walk. He doesn't respect you, your time, and your investment. And he will never live up to your expectations. He's what is known as the "avoidant type," one of those people who cycles through relationships very quickly. It's not as if they don't want to be in a relationship; they simply don't have the capacity for love.

It's a dilemma for many single, successful women who think they've been choosing the wrong men over and over again—and maybe they have. Just when you think you have met the one you really like, he disappears on you! You have read the "rule book" and followed every step there is in making sure you were not the one initiating the dating process. And you could swear he was head-over-heels crazy about you!

DATING IS NOT A WALK IN THE PARK

It's a sorting process. For most women, it actually is a frustrating experience. Many of your dates will be disappointments, and there will be days when you're ready to throw in the towel and swear celibacy. But if you go in knowing that and being patient with yourself, managing your frustrations and willing to stay open and curious anyway, then it doesn't have to be such a dreadful and daunting process.

It's almost never love at first sight as most women don't know that they are even attracted to a man until the fourth, fifth, or sixth date when they've heard enough, seen enough, met his friends, watched him interact with others, and then all of a sudden, a lightbulb goes off. And when it does, it's probably a healthier, happier love. Women fall in love between their ears. They have to sort men based mostly on their beliefs and expectations. Men, on the other hand, fall in love much more quickly. They are more visual beings, and they do have that initial physical reaction. For men, love and sex are deeply intertwined. For women, it's more about the heart-and-soul emotional connection of love, which takes a little longer to develop.

In the absence of any red flags, do give him another chance. Sometimes, the real first date is the second date. Some men are shy and don't really open up during the first few encounters.

DATING IS LIKE TREASURE-HUNTING

Love comes to us in different, unexpected packages. Be open. To enjoy the dating process, it's best if you go with the mind-set of just making friends first. Ask questions, be curious, get to know him. Questions you ask on the first few dates are basic ones, nothing too personal, because you're in the initial stages of getting to know him. You don't want to jump the gun and get personal by asking if he wants to get married, and how many children he wants to have, and so on. Don't do it. You're just feeling him out and assessing his character and seeing if it feels good to be with him. Ultimately, you may decide to just become good friends, and perhaps his best friend or his brother may be "the one" for you. At least by giving him a chance, you're opening the door for your paths to cross, and you will eventually meet your soul mate.

So often on a date, our minds are wandering, and we're looking into the future: "Is he the one, my soul mate?" "What can I do to know for sure?" "What's going to happen next?" We power through our date, and we're ready to jump to the wedding before we've even experienced kissing him. Slow down and lean back, experience the moment, be in your "feeling self," enjoy the connection.

The first thing to do when you meet a man and when you're dating is to understand what you're dealing with. Who is he in his behavior? How you know if someone's a good person or not is in his behavior—where he spends his time, money, and resources, his energy, what he concentrates most of his efforts on, how he talks and interacts with others. What are his values? Pay close attention to his behavior and discover who he is by observing his actions and by his responses in your interactions with each other.

Learn to ask for things that matter to you and for what you need in the relationship early on in the dating game. It's not wrong to ask, and it's never too much. It actually comes across as a sign of strength on your part and conveys confidence and assuredness in your femininity. Don't be afraid to test the waters.

DATING IS A DISCOVERY PROCESS

Go into it from an open place of curiosity. Be curious about people and be interested in getting to know them without an agenda. You're looking for a life partner, and you need to take time to know that he is someone who has the capacity to make you happy and be in the relationship with you for the long haul.

Conscious men are everywhere. When you're on a path of doing what you love, following your purpose, expanding your life, and getting outside your comfort zone, that is when "synchronicities" take place. All of a sudden, your path crosses with people who are on a similar journey, who are also trying to create an extraordinary life as you are. They are men who are constantly evolving, who are on a quest of bettering themselves in a positive way. Once you get "on purpose," you start recognizing the ones worth dating and those who resonate with your vision of a soul mate.

The most important golden rule is to really trust your instincts to be able to recognize insecurity and inauthenticity in the person you're dating. You're more susceptible to trusting people who initially seem sincere and are outwardly attractive, and even though something may happen, and there could be a lot of red flags telling you to walk the other way, you totally ignore that voice due to this very huge biological force called "attraction." Remember, though, that you're looking for a long-term healthy relationship, not just a casual fling.

IS HE A "KEEPER"?

How can you tell if you've met a conscious man, one about whom you can say with confidence, "He is a keeper"?

1. He is genuinely interested in knowing you: your needs and your wants, your desires, and what makes you happy.
2. He's someone with whom you can successfully talk through things and problems and he doesn't get defensive.
3. He's open, willing, and eager to learn and grow, to look at himself, to be a better human being.
4. He's attractive to you and there is chemistry between the two of you.
5. He doesn't shy away from tough conversations.
6. He's open-minded and not hypersensitive to anything that might be construed as criticism.
7. You have a shared vision of the future, and you really feel that vision is aligned.
8. He understands and respects your standards and your requirements and is willing to abide by the rules you have set in your relationship.
9. He deals with conflicts in a loving way to find a common ground in a disagreement.
10. He's able to express emotions, including sadness and fear, in a healthy way.
11. He's cultivated the ability to choose how he wants to respond. He doesn't react and fly off the

handle, seemingly controlled by circumstances and situations around him.

12. He is a "creator."

13. He is an honest person and has integrity.

14. He calls you when he says he is going to. He makes plans and respects and appreciates your time and makes sure that he never makes you wait. And if he is late, he makes sure to let you know.

15. He offers to pay when he takes you out on a date, showing you that he is capable of providing for your needs.

16. He introduces you proudly to his family, friends, and coworkers and lets them know how important you are in his life.

17. He talks about his past relationships, his friends, colleagues, and his family with respect.

18. He shows genuine love for you by willingly attending your family gatherings. And if you have children, then he is willing to consider being a part of your family by showing up with gifts and relating to them comfortably.

19. He would like you to date each other exclusively and makes it clear that he looks forward to planning a future with you.

20. He has a sense of aliveness and a connectedness to his spirit.

21. He's a "conscious" man who is aware of himself and his surroundings in any given moment.

22. He's not materialistic, but rather takes pleasure in giving back to the world and contributing to the planet and including others on his journey.

23. He's dependable and stays true to what and how he wants to be.

24. He does what he says he's going to do.

25. He is alert, aware, and awake. He is in charge of his life and is excited about it.

26. He's not a complainer but rather talks about learning something from each life situation.

If a man truly wants to be with you, you will know. You won't ever have to guess. If he's truly interested in you, you will hear from him, and he will make it *very* clear that he would like to spend time with you and get to know you better. He will be willing to put in the work. He's going to stick around and prove himself worthy of your time, your love, and your commitment.

THE MAN WHO SENDS MIXED SIGNALS

Inconsistency in a man can mean different things and may be a symptom of several unhealthy and unwanted dating flaws. Some men don't like consistency because it means commitment, which means a lot of closeness and responsibility for the other person's well-being.

There could be a number of reasons why he is sending mixed signals:

1. He is dating other women: Meaning that you are not the only one on his radar.

2. He is emotionally unavailable: Could be because he has been in a relationship and is getting over it, or he is separated or divorced, or even that he is totally preoccupied with his career and has no time for a relationship at this time.

3. He is unsure of what he wants: Perhaps he has dated different types of women and is attracted to this quality in one, that feature in another,

and he is confused. He does not want to make a decision and is unsure about you at this time.

4. He wants to have his cake and eat it, too: You are just a "time filler" as far as he is concerned. He is keeping you "on the line" while he checks out other women. He is just playing around.

5. He is only looking for sex: He only wants sex. That is all you mean to him. He doesn't have the capacity for the level of intimacy that you're craving, which means that he is not seriously interested in you.

6. He does not want commitment: He does not like the idea that he's responsible for someone else's well-being, and it's scary to him. He has this basic belief that you have to be self-sufficient and independent and that you need to take care of your own needs.

If you are receiving mixed signals from a man, don't put up with the nonsense thinking it is leading somewhere. If he shuts down, cuts you out, and doesn't allow you in, or responds with anger at the slightest chance, then he's not for you. Walk away.

When it comes to relationships, you're either a potential long-term possibility for the man or you're just a time-filler. You cannot be both. It is up to you to decipher the man's plans. It's up to you to set ground rules and guidelines, unless, of course, you're not expecting anything in particular from the man. If you don't set ground rules, you're letting him know up-front that you're just along for the ride, and then he knows he can call you whenever he wants and come by whenever it suits him. You are relinquishing your rights and allowing him to set the rules instead. However, if his plans are different from what yours are, do let him know without ado so you can move on.

Most men have commitment phobia. Marriage, to them, is a scary proposition. They know it's something they should be doing but don't really want to. They'd rather not shoulder responsibility and instead remain young and carefree. They want you and certainly don't want anyone else to have you, so they're only committing to lock you up. It's up to you to give him an ultimatum. Require him to marry you or set a date. Set some requirements and standards and enforce them. In the twenty-first-century courting scenario, you cannot use old-fashioned, twentieth-century logic, where it was assumed that if a man loved you, he would court you and then ask for your hand in marriage.

Understand your power and command respect just by the way you carry yourself. Men can sense that you're not playing games and will respect you for it. At the same time, your attitude is letting him know that you're looking for and are ready as well as appreciative of "the one" who can give you true, lasting love. You're the one in control. You decide the kind of relationship you want by the way you conduct yourself, by your image, the way you talk, and how you let men approach you. Make clear to him what you want and expect, what you're worth, and that you're not just his playmate.

You deserve clarity. You can tell if a guy is interested in you. If he's looking at you and actually "leaning toward" you, not leaning back and expecting you to come toward him, then he's the one who deserves your time and energy. On the contrary, if he's "leaning back," you don't want to chase him. Why waste all your years on a relationship that is not leading anywhere? No man should get any amount of your time if he's not into you—period. If he walks away, then let him. He's not the man you want anyway. And he's definitely not your soul mate.

In any dating scene, the best thing to do is let the man lead because it's the only way you'll know if he's really interested in you. If a man gives you his business card or his phone number, he is expecting you to pursue him. Don't accept his information, and tell him you're not comfortable calling men. Instead, give him yours, but only if he asks for it. Then wait for him to call you, to pursue you, to woo you, to wow you, because that is a man's role, not yours. Provide him with chasing space and let him take control.

Letting your date lead will help you gather important information about him. Give him a chance to show you how serious he is about you. How often does he call you or text you? How often does he want to see you? Is he consistent about it, or is he one of those who's happy to call but doesn't really bother to spend time connecting with you to build a solid relationship? If so, it's a sign of his lack of seriousness and interest in moving the relationship forward. If this is the case, don't waste your time. Best to move on.

When a man is not seriously interested in you, you have very little leverage to change him. Go on with life until you meet a man who is into you. The right romantic partner will consistently call, text, and want to see you. He will want to protect you and make you happy. He will appreciate you and go out of his way to make you his priority. A quality man who is interested in you will do his utmost to give you the world. Relationships not only take work but they also require that we work on ourselves. Being in a relationship helps us discover who we are so we can grow.

YOU DESERVE IT ALL

Being in a great soul mate relationship is about having a safe place to land. The person you are with really gets you; he loves you not only for all the things that are great about you but also for the parts of you that you hate about yourself. It's about getting your needs met and creating interdependency with each other. It's about allowing him to take care of you and being there for him when he needs you as well. If you're willing to be a good partner for each other, then it gives you the security and really affects your ability to explore, work, and be daring in the world.

Yes, good men are out there, and there are so many quality men to choose from. You will recognize one when you meet him. However, to let love in, you must know how to receive love. You cannot receive love from another who thinks you're wonderful if you also don't think you're wonderful. You hold up a mirror and attract those who reflect back to you your image and beliefs about yourself. Be your own beloved first. How you're treated will be in alignment with how you treat yourself.

You are good enough, and there is nothing you need to change. You don't need to lose weight, get a makeover, or drive a fancy car. You are perfect just as you are. It is not about you— so don't let anyone tell you any different.

Don't settle for just anyone and become another chapter in

the story about heartbreak. Put yourself first and be willing to fail. Don't be afraid to lose the man you are with if he is not right for you but rather seek out another who will love you and will want to go where you're going. Your intention is to get to a place where the "courtship" begins and "dating" is over. A good beginning almost certainly guarantees a good ending. Just be patient and know that you do deserve it all.

"The most alive moment comes when those who love each other meet each other's eyes and in what flows between them then.

To see your face in a crowd of others, or alone on a frightening street, I weep for that."

—Rumi

CHAPTER SEVEN

NO SEX WITHOUT COMMITMENT!

> "Sex is a part of love.
> You shouldn't go around doing
> it unless you are in love."
> —Bettie Page

Have you ever met a man who seemed to be "Mr. Right"? Everything about him seemed perfect. He was handsome, smart, a great conversationalist. He made you laugh, and you sensed a level of comfort and connection you had never before experienced.

It seemed he was really into you, and the chemistry was off the charts!

And so you slept with him very quickly after meeting him, but as it was happening, you got that sick and sinking feeling in the pit of your stomach, and you knew immediately it was a mistake. But the worst part was, even though you knew you should stop, you went ahead and did it anyway. Then he inexplicably disappeared from your life, and you were left hanging, wondering what was wrong with you.

When you feel chemistry, it's easy to get involved sexually. However, the misconception is in thinking that by attracting a man sexually, you will attract him emotionally as well, not understanding that men view a sexual connection and an emotional connection as two entirely different things.

Giving up sex to a man in the hopes that it will translate into a relationship, which is what they really want, is the biggest mistake women make in the dating scene. Having sex too soon can interfere with getting to know the real person. You want to make sure you're crazy about that person with your clothes on. It's too easy to become crazy about someone with your clothes off.

You want to be absolutely sure he is committed before investing your emotions into a relationship that may not pan out. It is best to wait to know each other better. It can make a huge difference, because by the time you do get together, you will be crazy for each other. Then you will know that he is the real deal.

There is a reason women should not become intimate with the men they are dating until they have a commitment. The hormone oxytocin, which is released in women when they become intimate, when they have sex with someone, tends to cloud their judgment. They will get more attached and bond with their partners at this point even though they may not be that into them nor have plans to be with them for the future.

DON'T HAVE SEX TOO QUICKLY

It's common knowledge that when you have sex too quickly, men tend to think there is nothing special about you and that you probably would offer yourself to anyone and everyone. This is not the woman they are looking to have a long-term relationship with. Men who will commit are out for far more than sex, and a woman who knows how to fulfill a man emotionally and sexually will be the one who captures his heart.

Know that most women bond through sex but men do not. Your body, after great sex, can tell you you're in love, but your brain is clearly letting you know he is wrong for you. Choosing men who are sexually available is not intimacy. Such men are generally not intimately available.

Assuming that you are looking for a soul mate and a long-term relationship (which I believe you are, or you wouldn't be reading this book), then you want to first make sure you're both ready to be in a committed relationship. Make clear that you *only* want to date each other, are not planning on dating anyone else, or having sex with anyone else.

It's best to refrain from casual sex until you're sure that you're both ready to be in a serious, committed relationship. Repeat: No sex without commitment because chances are you would be condemning your relationship to a sexual rather than a lovemaking experience. Know the difference between "getting laid," which is far different from "making love." As painful as saying no can be, remind yourself that your goal is to attract your soul mate and not a "fly-by-night" mate. Instead of engaging in sex, go out dancing, to the theater, on walks, until you know his agenda and he makes clear his intentions.

Men tend to want what they cannot have. If he thinks you're worth the wait, then he is going to stick around and prove to you he is serious about you. He is your man. But if those ground rules are too much and he walks away, then you will know he was just fishing. A man who loves you *will* wait for committed sex because he understands that a relationship worth having is all about bonding, falling in love, and being there for each other.

Let your dating partner know that you're looking for a commitment and you're not going to be sexual until you're in a monogamous relationship. Once you are both committed and are clear about taking the relationship to the next level, then talk openly about your sex history and STDs and make sure each one of you gets tested or has been tested. This is not just about disclosing your STD history; it's about getting your date to disclose his. You can never be too careful, because it's about you not catching anything. If he hems and haws, then it would serve you to walk away.

Women tend to trust the people they're attracted to even if

they have yet to prove they're trustworthy. They see and hear the red flags but step over them, giving priority to their feeling of attraction. Their biology tricks them into letting someone in and to start bonding with them. Attraction is important, of course. But it can also be dangerous because it can cause us to override our logic and ignore our instincts.

HOOKED!

Once you become intimate sexually, you are hooked. There is no turning back. You are shrouded in this trusting veil and you start making all the excuses to convince yourself that things are going to be just fine, everything will work out. So what if he doesn't call or show up when he says he's going to? So what if he's given you a clear picture that he was just looking for a good time, and that he had never been in good relationships before? Your relationship is different, or so you tell yourself.

You find yourself in this fragile state and convince yourself to tread lightly, that if you show your concern, the person will not love you, which may ruin the whole relationship. You start feeling that your needs are not valid, and that you want too much, that you're not being realistic or reasonable, so you wait and don't say anything. You overlook your partner's faults that could spell trouble down the road.

You wait and hope he can read your mind and pick up what your needs are and respond. You decide not to convey what you need, and as a result, you get upset when your date fails to behave in an ideal manner. *You* have failed to communicate effectively, and so when things don't work out, you blame yourself and believe that you're lacking, that you're not lovable, that you're not good enough, and that you should have known better. (Well, actually, you should have known better!)

Dating is not to be taken lightly if your ultimate desire is to meet your soul mate and to recognize him when you see him. The idea of going out into the world and finding this complete stranger and letting him into your life is a daunting one. To make this man your number-one person, your lifelong partner, well, that is a big task and requires your full presence and awareness. You will not only need to listen to what he says, but how he says it, and you will need to pay close attention to his behavior. How does he respond to you, and is he able to see and fulfill your needs?

SPOTTING THE WRONG MAN AND THE RIGHT ONE

You will really need to trust yourself and your instincts, paying attention to what you see rather than being mislead by a trusting veil. Express your needs in a secure way, and then see what unfolds. You still have some leeway and the choice to avoid sinking into the relationship in the early stages of the dating process.

However, once you become intimate with your date, then you are walking into a trap that can emotionally hurt and harm your self-worth if it does not work out. Bonding by sex becomes a very strong force that holds you together and makes it very hard to leave the relationship.

It is not easy when you have an intense attraction for someone to shake yourself awake and realize that even though you find him appealing, he is never going to be able to fulfill your needs. If you're asking for your needs to be met, and he cannot reciprocate, it would be better to walk away. The longer you stay in the relationship, the harder it becomes and the longer it takes to get over him.

The trick is to spot the unavailable, insincere, commitment-phobic men early on and move away quickly rather than get caught up in a lengthy drama and become so attached that it becomes painful to leave. Staying in a relationship that is not leading to anything fruitful robs you from meeting other people, people just like you who are also looking, who are available and have every quality that you seek, and who will really appreciate and value you.

Succumbing to a man's wish generally goes with his belief that you are surrendering to his maleness. Don't text, e-mail, or call. If you start to feel like you need to text him to find out what's going on, your feeling about having to text is already a red flag. You're not relaxed about the relationship, and you need to let go. You want to pay attention to how you feel when in his presence. Let him court you until you're on a more sure footing. Hold off on contacting him, and instead give him a chance to show you what his intentions are.

You want to date a man who is secure, who is dependable, one who is comfortable with sharing his feelings with you and letting you know what he thinks, how he feels. He understands your needs and responds to them, and you know that you are seen, that your needs are important to him. He is someone who has a shared vision for the future, someone with whom you really feel like your vision is aligned.

He is someone worth waiting for.

"When you do things from your soul you feel a river moving in you, a joy. When actions come from another section, the feeling disappears."

—Rumi

CHAPTER EIGHT

TRUST YOUR INTUITION

"I feel there are two people inside me . . . me and my intuition. If I go against her, she'll screw me every time. And if I follow her, we get along quite nicely."

—Kim Basinger

In the competitive world we live in, most women are leveling the playing field by cultivating a masculine power. We have become logical, linear thinkers, analyzing every scenario, twisting, molding, and controlling events in order to accomplish what we want to happen. We ignore and subdue that inner voice when it does not suit our desired outcome.

Certainly mastering this skill is wonderful and useful in many areas, especially in business. It's when we take this skill into manipulating our personal relationships that things can get messed up.

There are certain things that just cannot be controlled. To create authentic self-actualizing, growth-oriented, long-lasting, love-filled relationships, we need to go beyond what the eye can see. Trusting that inner knowing that you might feel but not necessarily know how to navigate is a skill that requires mindfulness and practice.

Alice had been dating Stan for almost two years before he proposed. Her wedding now only a month away, I could see she was having second thoughts. She said she was thinking of canceling her wedding. I asked her what had happened, and whether it was something they could work through.

Apparently, Alice caught her fiance cheating. Even though she felt something was clearly amiss when he started coming home later and later every night, she believed him when he told her his work was keeping him in the office. Until one day she happened to be in the area and decided she would go to his office and surprise him. The rest, as they say, is history . . .

Our intuitive voice plays a key role in giving us timely messages, messages that if we were to follow would save us from disappointments and heartache. More often than not, our intuition is right on, but we ignore the voice. Women have exceptional intuitions and sharp instincts. Our problems appear when we don't listen to them. Instead, we settle for someone who looks great on paper even when he makes us feel vaguely unsafe. Instant gratification is not what you're after, so stop making yourself an afterthought.

Not to confuse intuition with discomfort or irritation, although both are feelings one inevitably experiences in any relationship. Since we cannot expect everyone we consider for short—or long-term partnerships to be absolutely perfect, it's important to pay attention to things you really and absolutely can't deal with. Are these things you can live with five, ten, twenty years from now?

Compromise being the hallmark of a healthy relationship, traits that are minor irritants may need to be accepted and overlooked. Be clear to communicate about your priorities early on. What are your deal breakers? It is a question that is unique to each individual and is one to be contemplated and intuitively answered.

After all, soul mates come into our lives to reveal the deepest form of love there is while at the same time opening us up to the deepest form of healing. It's a magical process. When you have a true partner, you have a level of loving support that is incredible.

A soul mate relationship is not a walk in the park. If you're willing to do the work, willing to work on your growth as an individual and as a couple, then you will experience a deep level of security and safety. The sense of freedom and creativity that comes from that kind of love and devotion opens you up to be and accomplish things that you never thought possible.

Know that mere sexual attraction does not a soul mate make. Yes, chemistry is extremely important, but you must have a deep soul connection, compatibility, communication, and most important, a shared vision for the future. Without these, your relationship is doomed from the start. If he is lacking in any one area, he can certainly learn, so don't give up. But to do so, he must have an open heart and love and adore you and care for you enough to want to be a better partner to you.

However, you must be willing and open to overcoming some challenges with a commitment that sees the end goal. Such a challenge is the mind-set many men still have about the assumption of the role women should play in a relationship. Such men tend to marry women who will humor them, be available at every beck and call, and forgive them when they go astray.

If you're a woman who's been abused or has been in abusive relationships, it is common to subconsciously gravitate toward a man who is an abuser without knowing anything about him, because there is a frequency match and a familiarity with that kind of person that you are not even aware of. This is where you have to be conscious and discerning and where your intuition is needed to rescue you.

So, if your intuition is in overdrive, and you feel something is not right, do wait to consummate your relationship until you are secure in the commitment level in your man. If you pay attention to your gut feeling, you will not go wrong. Chemistry without compatibility can be deceiving. Save yourself the addiction and heartache from life's broken dreams.

RUN IN THE OTHER DIRECTION IF...

Here are a few instances when your intuition should be trusted. You intuitively know you should be running in the other direction because the relationship is doomed even before it has begun if:

1. You keep to yourself and never turn to him for comfort in times of need because you believe he will look upon you as weak and insecure. You're worried about letting him see this side of you and hide in the bathroom to shed your tears.

2. You feel that he loves his pet more than he is into you. He shows you less gentleness and caring than he does his pet.

3. At luncheon or dinner dates, he tends to control what you should order.

4. He has a habit of staring at you, which makes you feel uncomfortable even though he tells you it's because he cannot take his eyes off you and finds you so beautiful.

5. He's quiet and unresponsive, and it seems you're the only one making conversation and small talk.

6. You are uncomfortable with the way he behaves around his family and friends. He puts you down in front of them or is disrespectful to you or them, which embarrasses you.

7. Your basic goals for your future are different: you may want children but he doesn't; your religion and spiritual beliefs are different; you are a city girl but he prefers living in the country.

8. He has addictions and may indulge in too much alcohol on a daily basis or perhaps he gambles. But he comes across as sweet and exciting and involves you in these activities, trying to convince you they are perfectly normal.

9. You're not sexually attracted to him even though you find him very handsome. There is no chemistry, but you think perhaps you're analyzing too much, and it's just a matter of time, and you will soon feel differently.

10. You refrain from having deep conversations with him to air your grievances or bring up behavioral issues that bother you. You just want to avoid conflict at all costs.

11. You tend to check his e-mails and phones often because you don't trust him and are jealous of his friends and acquaintances who claim his attention and seem to be reaching out to him at all odd hours.

12. You have this strange, uncomfortable feeling that he's hiding things from you, and you cannot seem to shake it off.

If you find yourself struggling with any of the above, slow down. Rushing into a commitment such as marriage is never a wise idea. If you're still unsure and don't trust your intuition and want to give your relationship a chance to blossom, then perhaps it may be best to give yourself more time to get to know each other on a deeper level.

One never knows another person until one has lived with him for at least a couple of years, three at best. When you are in a new relationship, both partners are on their best behavior, revealing only the side that they want the other to see. However, given time, that façade falls off, and the true personalities and quirks come out of the woodwork.

All of a sudden, you realize there is another personality inside the person you have loved, and then you have a choice to either accept those shortcomings and love the person just the same or leave before it's too late. Don't ever think that you will "change" someone, because no matter how much you try, that is a most difficult, if not an impossible, task.

It is up to you to set a standard that requires that your man cherish you as a gentleman would. Share with him from the very beginning about what is most important to you and what you stand for. Then invite him in to experience your world and be open to understanding his world without bias.

Until you meet "the one," embrace the person standing in your own (frequently) impractical shoes. Look in the mirror. Yes, that's her. She's a loyal friend, and she will always be there for you. She is bedrock, the true, sure thing in this constantly changing world. She is your soul mate.

"Cease looking for flowers!
There blooms a garden in
your own home.

While you look for trinkets, the
treasure house awaits you in
your own being."

—*Rumi*

CHAPTER NINE

LOVE AND RELATIONSHIPS IN THE DIGITAL AGE

Thanks to technology, the way we experience love, intimacy, and connection has completely changed in this digital age. We are able to communicate instantaneously and more conveniently now than at any other time in history. How deep and meaningful or how shallow and fleeting these connections are can be a mystery, as more and more people are able to hide behind their conversations when communicating from cyberspace.

Meaningful conversations are now being replaced by rapid-fire texts and tweets; face-to-face interactions are replaced by Skype and Facebook. Social media connections, for the majority of us, are fleeting friendships. Try not updating your status for a few days and your so-called "friends" will have forgotten you already. Besides, how true are the events and statuses posted on these sites? Who is going to check, anyway? The society we live in can be called quite a "fake" society.

We tend to spend more time in front of a screen and less time with each other. We travel together, and yet we are each doing our own thing. We have become a vain society indeed, in that we are now immersed in our own needs and wants at the expense of our loved ones. It is not uncommon to see a couple apart, one busy taking selfies and the other just standing by the wayside, impatiently waiting and seemingly lost. They are traveling together, and yet they are not together. It seems the selfie craze is here to stay.

Nowhere was this more apparent than during my very recent trip to Hong Kong where I felt like I was scrambling to save myself from being injured from all the selfie sticks that had invaded the place. I kept bumping into people who were singularly focused on taking selfies of each other or themselves. From my hotel to a block down the famous Tsim Sha Shui Street, it was like a selfie minefield! I would be walking, and suddenly someone would stop in front of me. I would step back and bump into another selfie-obsessed person's back, and I was just like, "Crap, this is insane!"

It was quite a study of human nature and what a selfish society we seem to have become. We live in a culture of distraction and numbness. Many are so self-absorbed, complacent with the way things are going, desensitized and dissociated, and most have ceased to care. And I thought to myself: "What a struggle it must be for those in relationships, trying their best to get to know each other on a deeper level and to grow their love."

Oh, the vanity that love faces in this digital age!

It reminds me of the Greek mythology of Narcissus, a beautiful man who was fixated on himself and his physical appearance. Legend has it that he died by a lake because he was too obsessed and in love with his own reflection to go elsewhere. He stared at his reflection until he died.

This myth sheds light on the challenges relationships face in this modern day of superficiality and narcissism. We have become a society of people who are self-absorbed and oblivious of those who happen to be with us who may be trying to make conversation and get our undivided attention.

Perhaps you can relate. Let's say you are traveling together with your significant other in a far-off land to a beautiful country and surrounded by beautiful scenery, and you can't help but get carried away! Your partner is so excited to be with you, believing that you are there to spend quality time with him and bond.

But, lo and behold, the selfie stick comes between you two, and you are so singularly focused on primping and posing and taking your photos, running all over the place and stopping here, there, and everywhere, totally unaware of how you're making the other person feel. In the meantime, your fellow traveler is left in solitude, not included, and not invited to be a part of the fun you are having.

And so there you are, enjoying the trip thoroughly, clueless of how your actions are affecting your relationship. This continues for days, and before you know it, your partner has had enough and thinks this is never going to end, and he starts wondering again and again why he is there, and why he should be wasting his time stroking your ego.

Sound familiar?

All your partner wants of you is your involvement, your attention, and to share the journey with you. He craves to bond and wants to be involved in conversation with you. He wants to share his thoughts and observations and excitement with you. He wants to express his love and hopes to have it reciprocated.

But you, you are not sensitive to his feelings and expect him to play along with your wants. It's all about you. The trip, this life with him, is only about you and what would satisfy your ego and serve your needs.

Yes, the truth hurts!

Love in the digital age can be challenging. We have so many distractions that we connect with each other so very differently than we used to. Gone are the days when couples shared their time, their meals, and even had face-to-face deep conversations and invested in the art of deep listening.

Technology has affected how we experience love and how we communicate. We seem to text more than talk, we Skype instead of meeting face-to-face. We Facetime with our partners via the Internet, and we think we're spending quality time with them.

The way we connect today may have changed. The selfie culture may be here to stay. The digital age will see many more advances. But let us be mindful not to let technology ruin our chances of bonding with our partners or come between our relationships. Above all, let's stop allowing it to take over our lives and affect our long-term happiness with our loved ones.

Gadget detox is definitely the way to go, especially when you are with your loved ones and you know well that your relationship needs your focus and your full attention. Television, computers, phones, and tablets, especially in the bedroom, are destructive to relationships because they take your attention and focus away from quality time best spent in bonding and being intimate with your significant other. Rather than giving him your undivided attention and being present for each other, you are now immersed in affairs that are happening in cyberspace. Leave all your digital devices out of the bedroom in order to deeply connect and build your relationship with your partner.

Ultimately, you must decide: is your relationship important enough? Does it have priority over technology?

After all, you do want to nurture and grow your soul mate relationship—don't you?

"You can't upload love.
You can't download time.
You can't Google all
of life's answers.
You must actually
LIVE SOME OF YOUR LIFE."

—*Unknown*

CHAPTER TEN

GETTING BEYOND THE "IN LOVE" PHASE

You have "fallen in love," and you think he is perfect in every way. You are convinced he will make the ideal husband. This is it. He is the "real deal," and you are going to be happy forever with him. You are in love.

You let the other person know and hope the feeling is reciprocal. If it isn't, then you redouble your efforts to impress, and if you are lucky, you eventually win his love and start talking about marriage, because you believe that being "in love" is the necessary foundation of a successful and happy relationship.

When you are *in love* you are under the illusion that your beloved is perfect in every way. Even though others close to you may see his flaws, you ignore them because you know better. Your dreams have finally come true, and nothing and no one could ever come between you and your decision.

Most of us go through the "in love" phase and enter marriage by way of this experience. Our dreams, before our commitment, are of marital bliss. We are not totally naïve about potential differences that may occur within our union, but we claim certainty that we will overcome them by reaching agreements and making concessions for each other. We believe our love will last forever. Why shouldn't it?

It's time to pause now and be realistic.

Research shows that the average life span of a romantic obsession is two years. Eventually, all couples "in love" descend from the clouds and have a wake-up call. Those little traits that seemed so endearing in the beginning when you were in love now have become huge irritants: the hair in the sink, the toilet lid that never seems to be in place, the socks that are strewn all over the floor, the little white spots on the mirror, and the shoes that never seem to walk their way to the closet, and so on.

Welcome to the real world of relationships. When reality intrudes, even a look can hurt and a word can crush. Lovers can become bitter enemies, and the home a battlefield. Signing on the dotted line becomes more than the fanciful euphoria of having an "in love" experience.

My experience tells me that true love cannot begin until the "in love" experience has run its course. Under the influence of our initial obsession with each other, we choose to be kind and generous with each other, and we show up with our best selves. And we feel that is heaven. We feel secure and assured and committed to each other's well-being.

Stepping back now and being objective about the entire process will serve you in making wise choices. This is the time to be intentional and return to the real world where true love is not merely a state of infatuation. Love is a choice—the choice to look out for each other's interests and emotional as well as physical well-being; the choice to allow each other room to grow and reach his or her highest potential.

Wouldn't it be nice if you had conscious awareness and clarity of what exactly you want in a partner before jumping into a long-term, authentic relationship, especially marriage? To be married to a conscious man, you have to be a conscious woman.

WHAT IS "CONSCIOUS KNOWING"?

"Conscious knowing" means that you have sufficient self-awareness to make choices that empower you and honor your spirit and self. Rather than being impulsively driven, you can catch yourself and ask if the relationship serves your highest interest and is consistent to your commitment to yourself.

What exactly *do* women want in a partner?

Most of us grow up with set ideas of what our partners should be like. Many of those ideas are in fact unrealistic, dysfunctional, and usually based on how we have seen others behave at a time when we were most impressionable; sometimes we even acquired them through listening to fairy tales when we were very young. Or we feel compelled to settle for someone so we can be married at the right time rather than be married to the right person.

Reality is a far cry from those seeds that have been firmly planted in our minds. It is time to face the world of relationships as it truly is and realize that it is not without its own challenges. Any relationship you go into will require your conscious participation and consistent work. The intention is to hold your relationship to the level of Spirit and have as its basis a commitment to giving, so that each is secure in the love you bring to the union, thus allowing you to reach your highest potential in life.

Being aware of our needs is one of the most complex areas of life to fully understand and grasp. In order to gain clarity, there needs to be some soul searching and you need to take steps to figure out exactly what matters most to you. Be very clear about what you most need from your life partner and communicate early on to avoid misunderstandings. Let your values lead you to your perfect life partner.

Make a list of the inner qualities you would like to see in your "ideal" partner and be clear about which of those are most important to you so that you may go out and attract as well as recognize him when you do meet.

Just as when you decide to purchase a car—you study the different options available in the marketplace before coming to a decision and committing to making the purchase—so it is with a partner you want to spend your life with. Wouldn't you spend a little time to reflect on the qualities you would like in him as well as that car you bought?

The following exercises will help you gain awareness and clarity that will enable you to see, attract, draw in, and create the loving, conscious relationship you yearn for:

1. **YOUR PAST RELATIONSHIPS ARE YOUR BEST LESSONS.**

   Not that you want to dwell on the past, but looking back to see what did or did not work can help propel you to move forward with awareness. To have clarity of your past is the key to future success. I suggest you carve out some quiet time to contemplate, meditate, and, with a notebook and pen in hand, start writing. Be honest with yourself and go back over past relationships, no matter how brief or how long they were—how good, bad, or ugly.

   What was it that you loved about those previous partners? What did they do that made you happy and lit you up? Note the brilliant moments in each of those relationships and ask, "What were those? Great, I want more of that." What struggles and frustrations did you experience? Look back on those as well and note how your relationships were affected when "reality" set in and the initial romantic feelings faded. What was your role in triggering those behaviors and reactions?

   Then ask, "What is it that I'm looking for now?"

   This exercise is not meant to cause you angst or turmoil but rather to give you clarity and focus. Get real about your past experiences. You may notice a pattern emerge, one that may have followed you from one relationship to another. Perhaps this is an indication that you need to do some inner work before diving into another relationship or commitment.

Slower is better. Take your time. By reflecting and seeing what you need to do differently in order to grow and improve, by doing some inner self-work, you can bring a wholehearted person into your relationship. Deal with your personal issues before pursuing a new relationship. At the end of the day, the only one you have control of in a relationship is *you*.

2. **QUIET CONTEMPLATION.**

Take some time to meditate, slow down, and breathe. When the mind is empty, space is created between thought, action, and reaction, which helps ground us and brings clarity. The daily hustle and bustle of life can wrap us up in "overwhelm" mode, so much so that we lose sight of our true selves. Allow your intuition to save you from heartaches. Meditation and quiet time enable us to see life and people more objectively and help us make better decisions of what we want and need in life and in our relationships.

When was the last time you sat and did absolutely nothing for at least half an hour? Give it a try. Even if it feels uncomfortable, perhaps even excruciating at first. You may be overcome with anxiety, and memories of your past relationships may come flooding in. Be present with these emotions and just breathe. Acknowledge your feelings and give yourself permission to feel and process. A clear mind allows for clear intentions. By setting your intention to the kind of person you want to attract, you are sending out a signal to the Universe to bring someone with the right set of qualities to you.

3. **LOVING YOURSELF.**

   It's very common to put pressure on ourselves to find the perfect partner and forget the fact that the most important relationship we can have is with ourselves. Be gentle with yourself and take care of yourself first. Practice self-care; nurture yourself and do what makes you come alive and feel appreciated. Pamper yourself with spa treatments, gifts, and flowers. Go for nature walks or hikes. Anything that will enhance your self-esteem, contribute to a healthy self-image, and increase self-love is worth your time and attention. It is not selfish to do so.

   How can you give to others what you cannot give to yourself? Healing from any pains of the past, learning to take care of yourself, and overcoming your fears and preset expectations are all part and parcel of the process that will lead you to your ultimate goal. When you exude self-confidence, self-appreciation, and self-love, the other in your relationship can sense it. A man will only treat you the way you treat yourself. So love yourself completely. With practice and time, this is truly possible.

4. **LEARN TO RECEIVE.**

   We are always trying to prove our lovability by constantly giving. We tell ourselves that if only others knew how much love we had to give they would love us. Oftentimes, we give and give and go into sacrifice mode because we believe that we can buy love, that our partner will love us more if only we give more. As a result, we feel depleted, and sooner or later that feeling of resentment sets in.

   Learning to receive is like a muscle you have to develop. To help develop this muscle initially, you might consider getting a pet, because cats and dogs are wonderful at giving unconditional love. Say thank you for the love you receive from them. Start changing your internal dialogue and observe how you talk to yourself so that you can change your conversation. You could start with something as simple as, "I love and approve and accept myself just as I am. I am loved. The men in my life are loving me respectfully and unconditionally." Be among friends and family who love you and open up to receive their love without feeling like you have to do anything to get or earn the love. Stand in the sunshine and feel the love of the sun. The poet Hafiz said it beautifully: "Even after all this time, the sun never says to the earth, 'You owe me.' Look what happens with a love like that. It lights up the whole sky."

5. **LISTENING TO LEARN.**

    The path to heightened intimacy and lasting love requires mastering this skill. The way men think, communicate, and behave is different from how women go about these. Listening deeply to understand your partner and his needs is the path to deep-seated love and intimacy. Before you can get to that place, you must practice deep listening. Watch yourself when you are around people, whether they are friends, family, or colleagues. Do you allow them to speak their thoughts and really hear what they are saying? Or do you interrupt them to get your point across? You may learn something if you would just hear what is being said. Deep listening can help strengthen any relationship, and it starts with you.

6. **LOOK AROUND YOU.**

    Everybody needs an iconic couple to look up to, a couple who you feel has the kind of marriage you want. Perhaps there are people in your circle—

your family, friends, and even coworkers—who inspire you because of the love they share with their partners. If you don't personally know anyone, then pick some couples out in the world that you admire. What is it they do differently that keeps their relationship strong? Look around at the men in your life who you respect and admire; what are the characteristics that you see and wish for yourself? What do they bring into your friendship, your relationships, that you would like to see in a potential partner? Sometimes the answers are staring us right in the face and we don't even see them. When you are open and intentional, you will see that the Universe is showing you brilliant, extraordinary, fulfilling, passionate love that is out there because it exists, and it can exist for you. It is your job to see it and celebrate it. As you assess and come to some conclusions, ask yourself honestly: "Is this true?" "Is this possible?"

Remove your rose-colored glasses and accept the reality that the myth there is a "perfect" partner out there is just that—a myth. There is, however, a partner who is perfect *for you*. The degree to which your partner matches your vision of your ideal often determines the success of your relationship for the long term.

You can make choices regarding the fate of your relationship based on *reality* instead of what you *wish* it to be. A relationship consists of two whole individuals. Rather than looking at another to complete you, look for someone who complements you and your shared values.

And until you are clear about who you are, you cannot be clear about the person you really want to draw into your life.

Be love.

"The quieter you
become
The more you
are able to hear."

—Rumi

CHAPTER ELEVEN

IS HE "THE ONE"?

You have finally met someone you feel has truly earned the right to share your open heart, someone you are comfortable enough with to bare your less-pretty side, someone you feel safe with and trust enough to be vulnerable and share your scariest stuff with.

How can you know for sure he is "The One"? Can you be real and authentic with him and honestly say:

- He is my best friend, and I am comfortable about sharing my deepest, darkest secrets with him, knowing that he will not judge me.

- He really "sees" me for all that I truly am, not just what I represent.

- I'm attracted to him beyond his physical form and love him emotionally and realistically, at the "soul level."

- When we are far apart, I miss my best friend, and not just a companion.

- Even when we are not together, we have an understanding and really respect the foundation of faithfulness we have built between us. I would never go astray or hurt him, and I know he would never stray or hurt me.
- I trust him completely, and I know for sure that it is mutual and absolute.
- Being with him makes me want to be a better person and makes me feel stronger and more confident.
- I appreciate him in my life and know we will face challenges in our life together. However, I am confident about facing those challenges with him by my side.
- He shares my values and my vision for life, as I do his.
- With him, I can be completely myself.
- I can imagine life with him even when we are old and feeble, because of the kindness and caring we feel for each other.
- I am interested in supporting him in realizing his dreams and goals, and I know he will do the same for me.
- We are able to discuss our differences and frustrations with each other when they come up without getting into an argument.
- We never carry a grudge overnight and resolve all issues before they fester and get out of control.
- His strengths have rubbed off on me as I'm sure mine have on him. I am a better person around him.
- I love watching him when he is sleeping and feel so much love and tenderness toward him and am grateful for him in my life.

- I am not shy about expressing my feelings, dreams and ambitions because I know he always supports me.

- When we do have disagreements, we agree to disagree without any ill feelings.

- I am well aware that we do have differences that we may never agree on, no matter what. We understand this is very normal among people of the opposite sex and have agreed to accept them as such.

- We do not repeat or remind each other of things gone wrong or of each other's shortcomings.

- We enjoy and appreciate the company of our families and communicate with them with the utmost patience and reverence.

- We enjoy hanging out with the same group of people, and we have mutual friends whose company we enjoy together.

- I am fully aware that we are totally independent beings and that my happiness is not dependent on him. I also know that we could survive without each other but choose not to because we are content with, and love, each other.

- Even though he frustrates me sometimes (as I must frustrate him), I look past those instances and do not dwell or give much importance to them. At these times, we feel comfortable discussing our issues without harboring any grudges.

- We have been together long enough and know each other well enough that we would never attempt to change each other. We accept each other just the way we are, "for better or for worse."

- I am in this relationship for life, and so is he. We both believe in "Until death do us part."

- I am aware of his financial situation, as he is mine, and we respect each other's property. Money is not the reason for our relationship.

- Anything about our past is an open book, and we recognize that it has no impact on our present or our future together.

- We respect each other's religion and spirituality and agree to never encroach on one another's beliefs nor force the other to our way of thinking or our beliefs.

- I am well aware that things will not always be perfect, easy, or effortless. Nevertheless, we are committed to resolving our differences in a kind and loving manner and working through them.

- Our relationship has never been about "me," but always about "we."

- We love sharing everything and feel so much joy knowing that our lives are sweeter and better for that.

- We take time for each other, to listen deeply to each other, and enjoy sharing our days and our meals.

- He is my biggest fan, as I am his.

Any relationship that is based on this checklist is one of utmost integrity. It takes a lot of discernment and many dates to really tell if you are meant for each other. Make sure you're on the same page before giving your all, especially when it comes to sex, as people tend to have sex too quickly nowadays. Before you do so, it is best to make sure that you're both committed and willing to be monogamous and give your relationship a fighting chance.

Your intuition will let you know if he is "The One." Love will thrive and grow into a joyous and sacred union when you come from a place of inner stillness and connection; when you change within yourself the aspects of your inner world you don't like, you're coming from a place of selflessness, confidence, and safety. Create an internal space of peace, calm, and compassion. People can sense that. You are putting out into the world the energy you wish to receive back—that of love, support, compassion, and positivity.

Be ready to give of yourself openly and without any barriers. All you need to do is wait with confidence. Divine Timing plays a role in uniting you with your soul mate. While you may be absolutely ready for him, the Universe/Karma/God may have picked out the most perfect person for you, but it's not yet time for you to meet each other.

So, be patient and trust. Love yourself and your life where you are at this very moment. Share the love that is overflowing from inside you with your family, friends, and people you are surrounded with, and work on making sure you have released all the barriers to love within yourself. Perhaps you have still to forgive someone: perhaps even yourself? The time will come when you finally meet your soul mate, and you will experience the dynamic, amazing, intimate, passionate, incredible love you have been yearning for. You will then discover that it was all worth the wait, and the agony will turn to ecstasy.

> "Few have the strength to be a real Hero.
> That rare man or woman who
> always keeps their word.
> Even an angel needs rest.
> Integrity creates a body so vast
> A thousand winged ones will plead,
> 'May I lay my cheek against you?'"
>
> —*Hafiz*

PART III

Learning the Soul Mate Language

CHAPTER TWELVE

HOW WELL DO YOU KNOW YOUR PARTNER?

It's easy to get carried away by all the attention showered upon you shortly after you meet that special someone that you rush into a long-term commitment, even marriage. You feel sure he is the one who will make you happy and give you the unconditional kind of love you have been searching for.

THE HOOKUP, BREAKUP GENERATION

Here's a scenario you may be able to relate to:

You meet someone you're instantly attracted to.

You've been out with a few men and things never quite worked out, but for now, you're content to just hang out and have some fun. Who knows, he may even end up being "The One" for you. In fact, you're quite convinced he has potential. You see each other frequently in the first few weeks. You text and you call all day long. Your every moment is spent thinking of him, dreaming about him. He's all you can talk about with your friends and coworkers and anyone else whose ear you have. You know almost nothing about your date, and you don't really care. For now, this feels good. Really good!

Welcome to the modern world of dating, where instant gratification and "the future be damned" attitude prevails. We're the hookup, breakup generation. We have commitment phobia. We get into relationships at the slightest attraction and step away the moment we get bored. We date a lot of people but rarely give any of them a real chance. We are in too much of a hurry and don't particularly care to get to know the real person we're dating because it "doesn't matter."

Technology prevails in our relationships, so much so that our physical presence has been replaced by Skype, Snapchat, texts, and voice messages. We share so much of each other that there is nothing left to talk about when we do get together. We like to think we're different than everyone else, that we're "modern." We're into the temporary-fulfillment business, and getting laid is the new getting drunk. We think sex is love, so we have sex first, and if it feels good, we decide that it must be love.

And having determined this must be "love," we don't want to rock the boat. We're too afraid to cover hot-button topics for fear that he may walk. We're the practical generation that runs by logic alone. We just want to enjoy, loyalty be damned. We don't even value long-term relationships anymore.

CONSCIOUS DATING

But you, you're dating a guy who you're pretty certain may be "The One." You would like your relationship to transpire into something more meaningful. Would you not rather date *consciously*? If you answered yes, then wouldn't it help to know at least some of the basics about your date's inner world?

- What does he think of you?
- What does he feel about you?
- Who are his best friends?
- How does he treat his friends?
- Is he looking for a long-term relationship?
- What's his relationship with his parents and family like?
- What are his passions?
- What are his short-term and long-term goals?
- What are his life dreams?
- What is his basic philosophy of life?
- Is there fire and passion in his interactions with you?
- Does he appreciate you?
- Would you say he is your best friend?
- Is he giving and generous?
- How does he treat the waiters/waitresses at restaurants?
- Is he helpful, the kind of person you can count on when in need?
- Is he a problem-solver?

- Do you mesh well on your basic goals and values?
- Is he willing to wait patiently until you feel confident you are ready to be intimate with him?
- What's boring about his life?
- Which relatives does he like the least?
- How does he answer calls to people he doesn't really want to talk to?
- What's the number he's not sharing?
- How does he feel about children?
- Is he fun to be with?
- What are his hobbies?
- Is he dating you exclusively?

It's crucial to have at least three to five dates with an appropriate prospect. It is practically impossible to recognize your soul mate on the first date. There is a big difference between the sexes and the way we commit.

For a man to commit, he looks at you and hears the things you talk about, he assesses your feelings, your values, and your dreams before he is satisfied with the entire package you come in. He accepts everything about you even though there may be things that he wishes were not so. He chooses you by making the assumption that you are the best you will ever be in all ways, and he is fine with that.

However, women are the opposite. They can feel attracted in seconds but their commitment process is slower. They learn about a man one quality at a time and accept it as they get to know him. The things they don't like they believe they can negotiate, but if they get to the point where they know there is enough potential, they commit. Men rarely get accepted for who they are because women always want to change them.

The following are some basic areas about the life of your date you may wish to know before committing to a relationship:

1. **FAMILY.**

    How well do you know his family, assuming he has one? What's his relationship with his parents and his family like? It is said that you can tell how a man will treat you by the way he treats his mother. Does he respect her and care for her well-being? Does he introduce you to his parents and include you in his family gatherings? Does he respect you in their presence, and is he courteous to you and your needs?

2. **CAREER.**

    Do you know what he does for a living? Does he share with you at least a little of what he does and how his days are? Alternatively, does he take interest in your own career path and is he supportive of you? Is he interested to hear about your days, your goals, and your dreams?

3. **FINANCIAL.**

    Is he financially sound and responsible? Is he the type of person who likes to splurge, spend more than his means? Is he tight with his money, expecting you to pay for everything, not sharing? Alternatively, is he generous, or is he always counting every dollar and nervous about every little expense? Does he make excuses that he has forgotten his wallet and expect you to bail him out at the last minute (trust me, this happens!)? Even if your partner is not rich, he can be responsible and careful without being "cheap"! Can you communicate honestly about your expectations on sharing expenses, savings, joint tax return filings, and so on?

4. **SOCIAL.**

   Does he have friends, and do you know who they are? Are they kind, decent, generous, fun, and caring? Or is he a loner, expecting you, and only you, to fulfill his needs for companionship? Is he comfortable and does he allow you to spend time with your own family and friends, away from him occasionally? Or is he constantly monitoring your calls and your time, and is he jealous of your connections?

5. **EMOTIONAL.**

   How stable is he emotionally? For all you know, he may be a psychopath or a sociopath. Living together for the first two or three years will probably reveal his character. But then again, it might not! As difficult and preposterous as it sounds, it may behoove you to dig a little into his past and other long-term relationships, including any previous marriages and how they ended. Better still, if possible, get together with his ex-spouse or ex-girlfriend for a little tête-à-tête and see if they have amazing and wonderful things to say about their relationship. Not easy, but recommended.

6. **TOLERANCE LEVEL.**

   How tolerant and accepting is he of your quirks and shortcomings? Does he blow steam at the slightest aggravation or inconvenience?

7. **RESPECT.**

   How does he treat you in private, in public, or when among your friends and family? Does he give you respect and consideration and make you feel cared for?

8. TOGETHER TIME.

How well do you get along when planning an event, be it a trip, a dinner out, a Sunday drive? Does he expect you to be ready within seconds so he can get his Sunday going at 6 a.m. without including you in his plans or giving you a chance to be better prepared?

9. ATTENTIVENESS.

Is he attentive to your needs? Is he a sensitive human being who actually cares about you and what makes you happy? Does he communicate to you where he would like your attention and focus? A fulfilling relationship is the result of making sure that each person is being cared for.

10. COMMUNICATION.

Is he a good communicator? And by the same token, are you one? So many couples share the same home, bed, bills, and family but find it difficult to speak honestly and openly with each other. For this reason, when things go awry, they need the assistance of a counselor to communicate what bothers them about their partner. Best to nip this in the bud, don't you think? Be up-front about your expectations and your shortfalls and seek each other's help in improving this area of your lives.

The best feeling in the whole wide world is to open our hearts and watch things finally fall into place after having watched them fall apart for so long.

Finding true love these days takes more effort and focus than ever before. Where you put your time and energy matters. You want to be smart and discerning, as well as intentional, so you recognize a man of character when you see one.

And when you do finally meet and recognize each other, then nurture the relationship into the best friendship ever, because true friendship is the key ingredient of a long-term, soul mate relationship.

It is this friendship that will take you to the point of saying, "I do."

*"But for us this day
is friends sitting together,
With silence shining
in our faces."*

—*Rumi*

CHAPTER THIRTEEN

WHAT DO YOU BRING TO THE RELATIONSHIP?

*R*esearch shows that a healthy, lasting relationship is attributed to two main ingredients: kindness and generosity.

To understand the qualities we would like in our partner, we need to arrive at a stage where we understand ourselves and our needs. This knowledge will help us avoid getting caught up in relationships with people who are not at the same stage of growth as we are or with those who are unable to give us what we yearn for.

The opposite is also true. Expecting your partner to keep giving you what you want in your relationship is not only detrimental to its success but also a selfish way of being.

Your soul mate relationship is your vehicle for deep and meaningful fulfillment. You can feel immense joy when you meet your partner's needs while at the same time honoring and not downplaying your own. It can give you a surge of energy that flows through all other areas of your life: your work, the way you approach challenges, and even your physical health.

BE AUTHENTIC—AND FEMININE!

Today's women have allowed the masculine energy to take over their lives. In the "busyness" of their daily lives, they are locked down into the *doing* mode, living in the "head" and being in the "mind." They have forgotten how to be soft and to receive, to practice opening to their feminine energy and allowing the man to be in his masculine energy and give. They do not know how to balance their masculine and feminine energies and have become so excited about their work and career path that it has become their identity. It's all they talk about on dates and among friends and in their most intimate moments. Many women are extremely successful but not fulfilled. In the relationship arena, they are actually very depleted, often feeling unworthy and powerless.

If you want your relationship to be extraordinary, then bring your most authentic part to every experience, whether it is being compassionate or nurturing or family-oriented. See yourself as the work of art that you are, a divine creation, a beautiful human being, and exude that energy, that knowing, so as to bring out your partner's nobility, inviting the best in him.

However, in order to do so, you must first take a trip down memory lane and look at past relationships:

- What worked and what didn't work?
- How did your past relationships make you feel, and how do you want to feel in your new relationship?
- What are your "must-haves" and your "deal breakers"?
- Have you reconciled with your past, and are you ready to move forward?
- As a result of all those experiences and challenges, who are you now and what matters most to you?
- What do you value most, and what is the life you want to have now?

Write down all your answers and read them over and over

again until you feel at peace with your past and ready to focus on your future. Carve out and create the time and space to be fully present and to give your all. Be clear about what you want in a relationship and what you are looking for in that special someone who will be a great lifelong partner. And mirror that.

You need to cultivate the qualities that are part of being a great partner, have a clear sense of your own worth, and know what you are bringing to the relationship. Take responsibility for your own actions and behavior and look honestly at how you are participating in this dance. Get help if you must. Instead of reading books on how to *fix* your partner, understand that relationships are not always about the other person. They are as much, or even more, about *you*.

Focus on what makes you feel good and what you can contribute to the good of another person's life rather than living a single-focused, goal-oriented life. Lean back and learn to receive instead of constantly pushing and forcing things to happen. Allow.

Realize that being happy and fulfilled, accepting and loving yourself, is paramount to the success of your relationship. When you come from that place, opportunities and synchronicities jump out at you, and you will radiate and become attractive to your partner, magnetizing him to you. Ultimately, you will realize that when it is more about you and less about him, and you are focused inward on improving yourself, you are capable of giving more.

QUALITIES YOU NEED TO BRING TO YOUR RELATIONSHIPS

Below are some of the qualities you need to give to your relationships:

1. **TRUST.**

    Trust is the glue that holds all relationships together. Feeling insecure in yourself or in your relationship, inventing problems, or assuming something is true when it is not will weigh you down and ultimately destroy your relationship.

To believe in your partner is the greatest compliment you can give him and will allow you to experience a friendship and closeness that is unsurpassed. How well do you trust your partner?

2. **HONESTY.**

   Open your heart to love and truth. Stop trying to read minds or assume what the other is thinking. Say what you mean and mean what you say. Be honest with every aspect of your relationship: about what's right, what you want in your relationship, how you want to be treated, and what needs to change. And if you have done something or behaved in a manner that you're not too proud of, then be honest and share that as well. Communicate openly and often. Lying, cheating, and twisting reality can be the undoing of any relationship. Honesty can help heal each other's wounds and support each other's strengths. How comfortable and honest are you when sharing your darkest, deepest fears, doubts, and secrets with your partner?

3. **ATTENTIVENESS.**

   Lack of attention can damage a relationship far more than we realize. Be courteous when your partner is speaking, pay careful attention, and stay in close touch with his words and feelings. Give your undivided attention to his needs and communicate openly on a regular basis. Hold off on answering phones, texting, and social media, and be fully present in your conversations. Are you making the effort to be wholeheartedly present and attentive when you are together?

4. **LOYALTY.**

   Stand by your partner, especially in the darkest moments of your lives. In sickness and in health, in times of happiness and in times of sorrow, lift him up when he is hurting, and allow him to shine when he needs it. How loyal are you? Are you happy to see your partner happy and successful? What about when he is sad and worried: do you stand by his side and comfort him?

5. **RESPONSIBILITY.**

   Take 100 percent responsibility for your actions and feelings and behavior. Start looking honestly at yourself and be clear about what the relationship needs from you. Take personal responsibility and learn how to become an amazing partner. When you are looking outward for fulfillment and trying to fit someone else into a box of your making, you will only find disappointment. You will get upset over any small thing that he did not perform and blame him for any action that did not conform to your standard and your vision. Stop blaming and complaining and move past the problem. Look in the mirror and ask yourself, "Where is my responsibility in this?" A shift needs to happen so that you can both co-create the loving, healthy relationship you want.

6. **JOYOUS ATTITUDE.**

   Joy is a very attractive attitude. It draws men to want to be with you. Even if you are just dating and you're not quite sure he's the right person for you, just enjoy the process. Enjoy the other person for what he is bringing to the relationship. When you come from a place of joy, you automatically open yourself up to receiving and allowing whatever wonderful thing might happen. Who knows, he could be "The One." You're allowing the other person to have the pleasant experience of getting to know you. When you're in a "feel-good" state, then life feels good, and you draw toward you more of the things that make you feel good. Keep raising your vibration and be receptive to attract the love you most desire.

7. **TEAMWORK.**

   Healthy relationships are all about teamwork. You will achieve harmony and loving connection when you meet your partner halfway. Bringing wholehearted passion, love, and teamwork will strengthen your relationship. The strength of the whole is dependent on the strength of each individual part. You can conquer the world together through your unity. A good relationship is about sharing ideas and enjoyable moments together. How well do you relate to your togetherness: in your daily lives at home, at work, during travels, when planning for family gatherings and holidays?

8. **ACCEPTANCE.**

   Stop looking for perfection in your partner. Don't judge your current relationship based on your past ones. Making comparisons between your past relationships and reminding your current partner of all the good—or the bad—that you had experienced in the past can be the kiss of death. Your past pains are not indicative of your current possibilities, so let them all go. There is no such thing as a perfect relationship, and even if everything seems perfect now, there will be periods of imperfection and disappointment. Accepting and dealing with each other's shortcomings is what makes for an ideal relationship. Appreciate your similarities and accept your differences. Are you able to let bygones be bygones and accept your partner exactly as he is? Or are you hell-bent on changing him and making him see your point of view in every situation?

9. **KINDNESS.**

Offer empathy. Be kind always. It is the challenges and the pain that we experience that connects us on the deepest level. We all go through moments where we need a listening ear, a kind word, a shoulder to cry on, or even someone who will just sit silently by our side when we need time to process. How present are you for your partner? Are you kind in your words, deeds, and actions toward him?

10. **GENEROSITY.**

Be generous: of your time, in sharing your ideas, your belongings, in your intimate relations, and in your social connections. Sharing is caring. Being generous with your partner can be a source of great joy, while withholding is the cause of great sorrow and failure in relationships. How generous are you?

11. **ADMIRATION.**

Unleash every resource you have to light him up. Be a raving fan. Be his cheerleader. Remind yourself of all that you did in the beginning of your relationship to meet his needs and to get him to want to be with you. Are you still doing those things? Your partner could be the best thing that ever happened to you. Why not let him know how much you appreciate and admire him?

12. LOVE OF SELF.

You become naturally more beautiful the more self-love you give to yourself. Unless you love and accept yourself, you cannot love and accept another. Relationships are simply mirrors: What you feel and who you are will be reflected back to you. Your acceptance of your partner reflects acceptance of yourself as you radiate that natural, divine feminine presence. When you open yourself to self-love, you will discover that you are not so perfect and love yourself anyway. Is it not time that you said to yourself: "I love you!"?

13. PRIDE IN APPEARANCE.

Even though you think you will overwhelm a man's senses by the way you dress, by looking and smelling good, by feeling and sounding good, and by your overall appearance, in reality, you do all these things because of the pride you take in how wonderful it makes *you* feel. When you feel good about yourself, enjoy the pleasure of your own beauty and your own sensuality, then you exude the confidence that makes you more attractive to your partner. Your power to transform a man's attention is based solely on what you think of yourself.

14. AUTHENTIC PRESENCE.

Be your authentic self. You don't need to pretend to be anyone else but you. Feel free to present your true nature to the relationship. The partner who is designed to come into your life is not perfect, and neither are you. You are perfect together in your imperfection. When you come together in your authenticity, your partner will love you and see you unconditionally.

15. AMIABLE PERSONALITY.

Men who are playing for keeps are more attracted to an amiable personality than by looks alone. A beautiful woman without a loving personality will drive her partner away, because in the long run, every man wants a woman who is lovable.

Relationships, the lasting kind, take time and patience, and you must be willing to put in the effort. Have you done your part?

> "It's your road and yours alone.
> Others may walk it with you,
> But no one can walk it for you."
>
> —Rumi

CHAPTER FOURTEEN

WHAT DO WOMEN WANT (IN THEIR MEN)?

"I could not have known what love is if I had never felt this longing. Anything done to excess becomes boring except this overflow that moves toward you."

—*Rumi*

ARE YOU STILL SEARCHING?

You are by now perhaps a little disheartened. You have met enough men out there, but you are still searching for the one who could possibly be a match for you, someone who will appreciate the creative, gifted, conscious, smart, successful you; someone who will love and support you, value and sincerely cherish you enough to want to be with you in a loving and caring lifelong relationship.

You have yet to meet a conscious man, one you can really connect with and be seen by, someone you can be your authentic self with, connect with spiritually and emotionally, who can partner with you financially, sexually, as best friends, and playmates on all levels.

To begin with, you must create space in your busy life and make it your priority to start your journey toward finding your soul mate; be out and about dating and mingling, meeting people. If you need help then get help so that you gain clarity in recognizing "The One" when you meet him and having the relationship evolve into the one relationship that really makes a difference in your life.

How are you showing up in your life? Do you feel when you look back at your life now, that some really great men have indeed already crossed your path, and had you only shown up differently, given them more time and effort, the relationships could have taken on a different level?

Stop hiding behind your justifications. The cost of waiting is too high, and time is passing by. Make a commitment now to be open and come from a place of curiosity. When you are not attached to perfection, you will be surprised who shows up for you.

You may have been looking for someone who has everything that you deem perfect. Does he look the way you want him to look? Is he well-off financially? Does he live in the house, drive the car, and maintain the lifestyle that you want to have? Does he have the standing in the community that is impressive enough? Do the numbers add up?

You are yearning for a man who has all these dimensions. What you may have experienced thus far is either a choice between men who are really strong and successful and capable but lack self-awareness and those who are not emotionally available and kind of self-involved, intimidating, dominant, and strong.

Perhaps you're disillusioned because you've met spiritual *and* conscious men who you thought had potential and were wonderful until you found out they were broke.

Perhaps you're more of a feminine woman whose energy

is more flowing, creative, expansive, and emotive. You find the alpha man attractive, and you want a nice guy who is assertive, who makes decisions, and who stands in his masculine energy, someone who is powerful but not controlling.

You may be an alpha woman who is extremely talented, smart, efficient, effective, and likes to control everything, including the men she finds herself in relationships with. You believe that being in control can protect you and prevent him from leaving you or cheating on you. But so far, every man you've dated has been turned off by your controlling demeanor, which is actually pushing away what you most desire. You could start by overcoming your fear and looking at ways to soften and invoke more of your feminine energy, or else decide that a more compliant man—who is softer, more passive, and who will allow you to be the dominant partner in the relationship—may better suit your alpha personality.

Regardless, the only way to be in love is to open your heart, and in the process, be willing to have it hurt.

ABSOLUTE PERFECTION DOES NOT EXIST

You've read about the romantic love that exists, and you wish for yourself that romance, someone with whom you can communicate well, someone from whom you can ask for help and get it, someone who will nurture and support you.

When one or another of these qualities is missing, you draw the conclusion that there is a lack in the Universe and your soul mate is not in your stars, at least not in this incarnation. So, you might as well resign yourself to being alone forever. Perhaps one really cannot have *everything*, so you say.

Not so fast!

These are merely stories in your head, stories you have made up that are very painful and confusing. You have convinced yourself they are true for you. But that is totally false, false because you are looking for absolute perfection, and absolute perfection does not exist. Even *you* are not perfect. But you are perfect enough for the person who is perfect for you. He may not have every single thing on your list of the qualities of a perfect soul mate, but if he has enough good qualities, then he may be a contender.

Soul mate love is not about wild and crazy passion, the in-the-heat-of-the-moment kind of feeling, but a tranquil love where you experience the deepest of friendships, where you feel like you can be open and vulnerable and discuss anything under the sun and know you will be heard and never judged. It's where he sees you and knows you, and he's compassionate and understanding and patient. Where you allow each other to grow and you support each other on your journeys. When you look into each other's eyes, you know you're home.

HAVE ABSOLUTE CLARITY

To begin with, you must have absolute clarity about what you want in your relationship, why you want it, and what it would feel like to have it. Get quiet and go deep within to gain clarity on what your soul is most calling for. Is everything you think you want in alignment with your true desires, or are these based on perhaps your mother's or your sister's or your friend's lists? Chasing things that aren't authentic to you just because this must be what you want because others have told you so will not ultimately keep you happy and give you joy.

This is about you and no one else. It's your life. Relationships are often mirrors that reflect our opinions of ourselves and our self-worth. You want to show up in your relationship in the same way you want someone to show up for you. If you love yourself, you automatically draw that love to you. Your existence is more than enough, and you are worthy of the most amazing love and true happiness. There is nothing and no one you need to control, or change, or make happen. You are allies; you each know that you are whole and complete in and of yourselves, but that you are also adding a tremendous good to each other's lives. Just be open and fully and completely your authentic self. This is called *healthy interdependence.*

The questions you should be asking yourself are: "Do I like him? Do I appreciate how he treats me? Does he appreciate how I treat him? Does he love and respect me? Do I love and respect him? Does he really see me? If we had children, would he make a good father? Would I want our children to be like him? Would I want to be more like him? Do I admire him enough?"

It is important to be clear on what your core desired *feeling* is in a relationship. Get clear on how you want to *feel* in love. Ask yourself, "How do I want to feel in life? How does he make me feel? What's most important for me to feel in the relationship?" Your clarity will help you attract the person who creates these feelings in you, and you will recognize him when you meet him.

A soul mate relationship is not all smooth sailing. There are issues that will come up and obstacles to overcome. But you have made a pact to grow together, whatever that may involve. What's most important is that you have a shared vision of your future together.

There is a soul mate for each one of us. The Universe is abundant. If you put forth a clear-enough request and hold that vision and believe in it at the very core of your being, feel that it is already so, your wishes will be answered.

Remember our discussion about the law of attraction in Chapter 4? The law does work. But it will only work if you are clear about your desires. What is it that you want in your partner? How do you want to feel in your relationship? Beware of mere physical attraction. The body can be deceiving. So, trust your intuition, your feelings, and give yourself time. Be cautious and get to know each other before taking any major steps.

As much as we keep hearing about our gender from men—that we're too complicated and mysterious, too fickle, somewhat vain and vague, too this and too much that—at the heart of every woman is the same yearning: that her love be reciprocated in the same way that she gives it, that her emotions be met with the same intensity that she brings to the relationship.

We may be a little more complex than men, but we reach for the same dream: a loving partner, a home, a happy life, and perhaps some children. We each want similar qualities in the person we commit to. We, as women, know exactly what we wish our partner would portray in the relationship. We want security and surety in our relationship that will allow us to be able to step out into the world with confidence. Knowing that you can depend on someone to be there for you, someone who provides safety and security, love and devotion, frees you on your own path to independence, to great success in your career and life.

Today's dating scene is more complicated than past

generations'. Infidelity and a short attention span along with the hit-and-split mentality that is rampant can make us jaded and lose our faith in ever finding the right partner. We brace ourselves for the worst and proceed with extreme caution, holding ourselves back, unwilling to share ourselves with just any man.

On the other extreme, we believe we must be aggressive in going after what we want. That is a fallacy. Aggressiveness stems from fear. To magnetize another, it is true that there needs to be focus and an intention and action to be taken. However, there also needs to be a stillness, an "allowing" to the action while being in your sensual power and fully immersed in your feminine energy. You are not being passive, but rather you are holding that energy and drawing him to you by creating the space for him to court you in his divine masculine energy. You are allowing him to do the seducing.

What a relief it is when we do stumble upon a true gentleman who exudes chivalry and shows us that he cares and that we matter by his smallest gestures and sincere actions and with romantic interest and undivided attention; a man who wants nothing more than to give to us, to make us happy, to stand with and for us, to protect us, to support us, to empower us to become the wholeness of who we are so that we get to experience the joy and the delight from that place.

Yes, the good ones are out there, so have heart and don't just settle for anyone who happens to come along. Chivalry is not dead. The right person is out there, and he will show up once you are clear. What are some of your must-haves, the deal breakers, things that are nonnegotiable on your personal soul mate wish list? Brainstorm and make your list, write down everything, even the materialistic things and the things that you would never share with anyone. Be clear and be willing and ready. You will attract what you are vibrationally ready to receive.

THE CHIVALROUS ACTS OF A CONSCIOUS MAN

A conscious man thinks nothing of performing these simple but chivalrous acts, as they are almost second nature to him. These subtle and meaningful gestures can melt our hearts.

1. **HE SENDS YOU FLOWERS.**

   Not just on Valentine's Day but at random and for no other reason than that he cherishes you. He picks up flowers on any given day and sends them to you, showing you that he is thinking of you and that he cares.

2. **WATCHES YOUR FAVORITE MOVIES WITH YOU.**

   When a man suffers through a "girly" movie with you just because he knows you will enjoy it, and he likes to see you happy, he is a keeper.

3. **OPENS THE CAR DOOR FOR YOU.**

   He walks around and opens your car door and waits patiently and lovingly until you are seated. And in the winter, he makes sure to turn on the engine and have your car seat heated because he cares about your comfort and well-being.

4. **FILLS UP YOUR CAR WITH GAS.**

   What a welcome surprise to know that your partner cares for you and wants to make sure that you have everything you need, including a full tank of gas to start your day.

5. **OFFERS YOU HIS JACKET WHEN IT'S COLD OUTSIDE.**

   How considerate of a man to offer his jacket and shield you from the cold—or better still, be kind and gentlemanly and hold your jacket out for you and help you into it. It shows his nurturing and caring personality.

6. **PULLS OUT YOUR CHAIR.**

   At a restaurant or anywhere before he seats himself, he makes sure to give you the courtesy and see you comfortably seated before seating himself.

7. **HE'S ROMANTIC.**

   Romantic love is so important to you, and he knows it. His actions and his words tell you how much he values you, and that in his eyes you are the most beautiful woman. By providing you romance, he helps support your feminine side, thus increasing your happiness.

8. **HE LIGHTS UP WHEN HE SEES YOU.**

   He lights up with adoration and is overflowing with love when you walk into the room. He is always excited to see and be with you. You feel surrounded in an exquisite field of love when you are with him.

9. **HE HAS WONDERFUL COMMUNICATION SKILLS.**

   He's engaging and intelligent. You have great conversations. You learn more and more about each other as you communicate. He is very respectful and gives you space to express yourself, and he respects your thoughts and feelings.

10. **INTRODUCES YOU TO HIS FRIENDS AND FAMILY.**

    You are no secret to his near and dear ones. He proudly introduces and includes you in all interactions with his family and friends, showing them you are an important part of his life. He professes you as his own, and he's putting everyone on notice by making clear his intentions for you. By showing his respect for you, he is subtly expecting them to respect you as well.

11. HE PROTECTS YOU.

He holds your hand when crossing the street and places himself on the outside of the sidewalk to protect you. Anyone who disrespects you or says or does anything offensive to upset you will be obliterated. He will keep you safe from harm at any cost because he cares for you.

12. SPENDS TIME WITH YOUR FAMILY AND FRIENDS GLADLY.

He believes in family, in building and nurturing relationships. He shows interest in your family, pays compliments to your mother's cooking, or participates in your family activities with enthusiasm. Small gestures, but they speak volumes.

13. SHARES HIS FOOD WITH YOU.

Just as with everything else you do together, he offers to share his food with you and even saves the last bite for you because he likes you so much.

14. HE DOES WHATEVER IT TAKES TO SEE YOU HAPPY.

There are times you say no to your partner when something does not feel right or ethical. When you say no to what you don't want, he finds the things you do want by experimenting and creating. He finds out what turns you on and does whatever it takes to see you happy.

15. HE CHERISHES YOU AND YOURS NO MATTER WHAT.

Even when they are irrational, irritating, and totally illogical, your partner cherishes your children, your animals, and your relatives and friends. He does this with a good attitude and a calm demeanor.

16. HE IS SUCCESSFUL IN HIS VOCATION.

He's excited and passionate about his work and is fulfilled by his job. He has mission and purpose and enjoys activities that give him joy. He's not looking at you as the source of his fulfillment, and he is financially secure.

17. HE RESPECTS YOU AND YOUR VOCATION.

He treats you with utmost respect and is supportive of your career, cheering you on to be the best you can be. He doesn't interfere with your wanting to express your wholeness. You are assured that you can have both a career and a loving partner without having to compromise one for the other.

18. HE PROVIDES FOR YOU.

He takes care of your needs, whether they are monetary or otherwise. Even if he cannot afford much, his efforts are what matter. He does what he can to make sure you are reasonably satisfied and that your needs are met. It gives him pleasure to see you happy.

19. HE SEES YOU.

We all crave to be seen. Rather than seeing just your outward beauty, he sees you as a human being. He sees your curiosity, your inquisitiveness, the way you talk, the way you listen and pay attention, the way you laugh. He's sensitive to your needs. He makes you feel appreciated for just being you and provides a level of emotional fulfillment that sustains your own self-actualization.

20. **HE IS COMPASSIONATE.**

    He is a conscious man who has tremendous capacity for love, compassion, and empathy, and enjoys being of service to others. He is considerate of you and your feelings and connects with you on a deep level. He listens deeply and is focused on you. He can empathize with all that you go through.

21. **HE'S DEPENDABLE.**

    He hears you, and when you're feeling emotional or upset or something is bothering you, he's by your side, assuring and comforting you. He comes through when he says he's going to do something or perform some task. He keeps his word.

22. **HE IS SOMEONE YOU CAN BE AUTHENTIC WITH.**

    You can safely reveal your innermost insecurities and be vulnerable without being afraid of being judged. He welcomes the authentic expression of who you are. He provides stability and strength. You can share what's going on in your inner world and be sure of his complete focus and emotional support. He seeks to try to understand you and your point of view with respect.

23. **HE HAS UNSHAKABLE INTEGRITY.**

    You know he's got your back. He makes you feel safe and he is committed to making you happy. He's like that with everyone in his life.

24. HE IS SPIRITUAL.

> He believes in God, the Higher Power, the Universe. He is honest and truthful and lives his life with congruency.

There is a wonderful man out there waiting for you to find him. He is looking for you, too. Open your eyes and your heart, show up, and be available by being vulnerable, open, and interested. Participate in life, be receptive, and trust in your power to manifest your soul mate.

Your core beliefs will be challenged, but that is the fun! Just allow. It doesn't mean that you're always going to attract the perfect man, and you may have to go through several to find him. Just know the Universe supports you in your transformation to a future where you may blossom and flourish in ways that you may have never expected or imagined and lead you to your true love.

All you need is one respectful, caring, and loving person to fill your life with joy and to cherish you in all ways. You recognize that you are coming from a level of self-sufficiency and are not looking to a man to make you whole, to make you fulfilled, but one whose behavior can take you higher than you can take yourself. He is your soul mate.

Who said chivalry is dead? When you meet a man who pays attention and shows such kindness and courtesy, it means that he is really into you. Allow yourself to be unconditionally loved for who you are, supported in who you're becoming. Your soul mate may not always think the way you do, but he will have similar values to yours. In fact, what creates attraction is the differences between the two of you.

Maybe there is no "perfect" man, but definitely the one who has close to all the previously listed qualities is as perfect as they come.

And because you are a real woman, you get to demand that he stand up and deliver!

> "Whatever love wants,
> it gets,
> Not next year,
> now."
>
> —Rumi

THE SOULMATE CHECKLIST

CHAPTER FIFTEEN

WHAT MAKES A WOMAN IRRESISTIBLE TO A MAN?

*Y*ou never get a second chance to make a first impression" may sound clichéd. But did you know that during the first five minutes of your meeting with a man, he has already formed an opinion of you?

Many times, we wish for the right people to come into our lives, and we don't understand why we can never seem to attract them. What exactly are men looking for in a woman? This is a question that seems to elude most single women.

It is New Year's Eve, and a group of us, all friends, are gathered around a cozy fire facing Lake Arrowhead on this chilly but clear night. There are many single, smart men in our group, and the conversation steers toward what exactly it is that single men are looking for in a woman. The universal feedback clearly indicates that the answer is actually quite simple.

Alain's story, as narrated here, encompasses everything that men initially find most attractive in a woman.

Alain happens to be at the Polo Lounge of the Beverly Hills Hotel on this Friday evening. He has just come out of a long and tedious meeting, and he is ready to spend a laid-back evening just listening to the wonderful live music and later get a bite to eat before going back to his bachelor pad.

Alain is single and in his late thirties. He has been so busy growing his law practice these past few years that he has not had time for any relationship. Some evenings, such as this one, he wishes he had someone significant to share his life with. His friends are all married now and weekends are starting to feel somewhat lonely. Even though he's been introduced to a few women, he just doesn't feel they are for him.

On this particular evening, he's seated at the bar savoring his glass of cabernet sauvignon, sipping slowly, deeply immersed in his thoughts. Just then, he looks up and sees a very attractive woman walk in and order a drink at the bar. He sees her profile; her silky brown hair is tucked behind one ear, and she's wearing a soft, lilac-colored dress. She turns to look at the crowd, and Alain sees her hazel-colored eyes and her bright warm smile. Their eyes lock. She's pretty and carries herself confidently. Alan doesn't look away and neither does she. This lasts for a nice, long moment.

He considers walking over to the end of the bar where she is standing, now with a girlfriend who has just joined her, and introducing himself. He wonders if she is single. He hopes she will not think he is one of those men who inevitably hang out at bars chasing women. He hesitates, feeling quite shy now.

He wonders, "What exactly am I looking for in a woman?" It's been far too long since he dated anyone, let alone met anyone with whom he felt as if the first meeting could turn into a first date. His past encounters have been quite disappointing. For a woman to capture his heart, he wishes for her to have these qualities:

- **Confidence**: She doesn't have a big ego, mind you. But she feels secure in who she is and assumes she is awesome in her own right. She commands respect merely by the way she carries herself. She knows how to set boundaries and take care of her emotional needs. She shows that she is genuinely interested in finding out what is also awesome about the man she has just met. Visual being that he is, little escapes his notice as he appreciates how she carries herself, the clothes she's wearing, her walk, her hair, her "all." Confidence in a woman is very attractive and actually very sexy.

- **Physical magnetism:** What initially attracts a man is body language through outer appearances. She is well groomed and takes pride in every detail of her appearance, not just the clothes she is wearing or the way she wears her hair and makeup. She looks both well dressed and sexually appealing and has the "little" things, like well-manicured nails, good oral hygiene, a soft and subtle scent instead of reeking of perfume. Men notice all the little details and appreciate a woman who takes care of her appearance from the inside out.

- **A tasteful sense of humor**: A woman who smiles shows that she is generally a happy person. She is not shallow and does not laugh too often or too long at what may not be funny enough. Nor does she agree too quickly before he has expressed any actual points or ideas, either. And above all, she is never sarcastically funny or makes jokes at her date's expense. She is sincere and skips the sharp-edged wit. A good sense of humor is a woman's greatest asset.

- **"Full-on" presence**: She is focused on what a man is saying instead of fidgeting with her napkin, her hair, or shuffling through other thoughts such as, "I wonder what he does?" or "How do I look?" or "Will he be the guy I marry?" Her mind is totally clear and she hears the words of the man she is with instead of being mentally distracted. She looks at him while he's talking and is really committed to listening. He can feel her attention, her eyes on his lips, and her reaction to the words he is saying. There is nothing more romantic than letting the man she is with know that she is totally present with him.

- **Passion**: She is passionate about herself, her beliefs, what's important to her in the world. She is passionate when sharing her ideas, her hobby, her job, her art, her family, or anything it is that she is into. It doesn't matter what it is that she's conveying. She's letting him know what she wants in life and what she's actively pursuing. When he hears her passion, he is able to understand her better and also know that she will support whatever it is that *he* may be passionate about.

- **Intelligence:** A woman who can hold a respectful, respectable, and intelligent conversation is admirable. She proves that she can hold her own in any setting, at any meeting, in a restaurant, or at any family event and gathering. She is a woman he is proud to introduce to his friends and family.

- **Independence**: Men admire a woman who has a fulfilling life, who has lots of friends, has activities that she loves to get involved in, whose work is very fulfilling to her, who is independent, and who does not depend on him for her happiness.

- **Appreciation:** Any woman who shows her appreciation for all that her partner does wins his heart. Acknowledgment and appreciation are the fuel a man runs on in a relationship. More than anything, he needs her to understand and validate him and to let him know that he makes her happy by all that he brings to the relationship.

- **Value**: Men like to know that they're providing something of great value to the relationship, a sense of mission and purpose. A woman who makes a man feel needed and valued makes him want to love and care for her more deeply.

- **Loyalty:** For men, love is loyalty. They appreciate a woman who will stand by them no matter what happens. This includes setbacks in life: for example, if his business sees a downturn and he cannot bring home as much as he used to, or if his health suffers and he needs her to stand by him and nurture him. If her loyalty is real and unimpeachable, she will have him for life.

- **Calm demeanor:** A healthy, masculine man is turned off by a woman who is too talkative or who brags about herself and her accomplishments. He cannot hold on to his masculinity in her presence and will either feel emasculated or leave. He appreciates a woman with a calm presence.

- **Knows how to receive**: She loves to feel cherished and pampered, to have the man open the car door for her, take care of her, hold her hand when crossing the streets, and to be attentive to her in restaurants and among friends and family. She feels nurtured and safe and protected, and her graciousness makes the man feel he is needed and valued. He sees through his actions that she's happy, and because she appreciates and acknowledges him, he feels like he has won her over.

- **Trust in her own opinion**: He respects a woman who knows and trusts in what she wants and is comfortable in expressing her opinions and her needs. Forming opinions of him based on what her friends or family think, mentally inviting people to sit on the judges' panel and perhaps disqualify him immediately after they meet is a big mistake. It does not give her a chance to get to know the real person he is. Many women have the habit of testing the man they meet on their very first date rather than giving themselves permission to discover what exactly they may like about each other.

Getting back to our story about Alain: Coming out of his reverie, he gets up to walk over to the woman at the bar, but he sees that she has already moved away with her friend and out the door. Another opportunity missed. He wonders if he will ever meet her again, and if so, will he hesitate or will he at least take a chance? What would he say to her if he could be with her now? Hopefully, he will be ready the next time he meets a woman he is attracted to.

The scene painted here clearly shows what draws men to want to know you better in the initial stages of courtship. A man who is courting is ready to commit soon after he meets you. He is drawn at first to your outward beauty, and within minutes of having a dialogue with you, he knows if you have potential. Then he begins to pursue you with dates, phone calls, and little gestures such as gifts, flowers, and cards. He is in essence saying that he has met a woman who could be his potential lover, wife, mother of his children, and he is committed to entering a long-term, monogamous relationship with you that may or may not culminate in a marriage.

It does not matter how good you are for each other. Until you understand what men are looking for in a woman, what drives and motivates them, what their priorities are, and what love means to them, your plans, your dreams, and your desires for a solid relationship may well be for nothing.

MEN LOVE WOMEN FOR WHO THEY ARE

Many women believe they have to be perfect to show up. Men—the genuine, loving kind—like women who are willing to show their flaws, who are available to receive love. They appreciate women who are transparent, vulnerable, and open. Men don't love us for what we *do*; they love us for who we *are*. Our state of being is what attracts them to love us, which is why it's so important for women to embrace and embody the essence of authentic, empowered femininity.

It's a myth that men are intimidated by a strong woman. In reality, it's not that men don't want an independent woman, but they want to feel they are of value and that they are needed for something. They want to feel like they are contributing added value in some way to the relationship and that you need them—not that you couldn't survive without them, but that they really add a tremendous amount to your life.

Men are also clueless for the most part, and since they don't come with mind-reading capabilities, they are looking at you to tell them what you like and dislike. Share with him, let him know, show him so that he can win with you. And when he does the things that you like, then acknowledge and appreciate him.

Men are simple beings. There are three main things that matter to them; it is their mission in life. Happy and fulfilled men are mainly driven by *who they are, what they do,* and *how much they make.* Stability is important to them because they want nothing more than to make sure they can provide for and protect their family.

Men want to feel needed and appreciated, and they want your loyalty. They want to impress you either by their resources, their history, their wit, or their intelligence. They need to think they can make you happy by giving you what you need—what they think you need. Their love is really as simple and as direct as this.

If you can lavish praise and let your partner win and be acknowledged—without feeling like you are losing your power—it makes you magnetic to his love. If you can make him feel he has your support in understanding his vision, focusing on his dreams, and implementing his plan—while you're nurturing him and letting him know how much you appreciate him—then the world is your oyster.

There is nothing a man will not do for you when he knows how much you care, that you are behind him and cheering him on.

> "I see my beauty in you,
> I become a mirror that cannot
> close its eyes to your longing."
>
> —Rumi

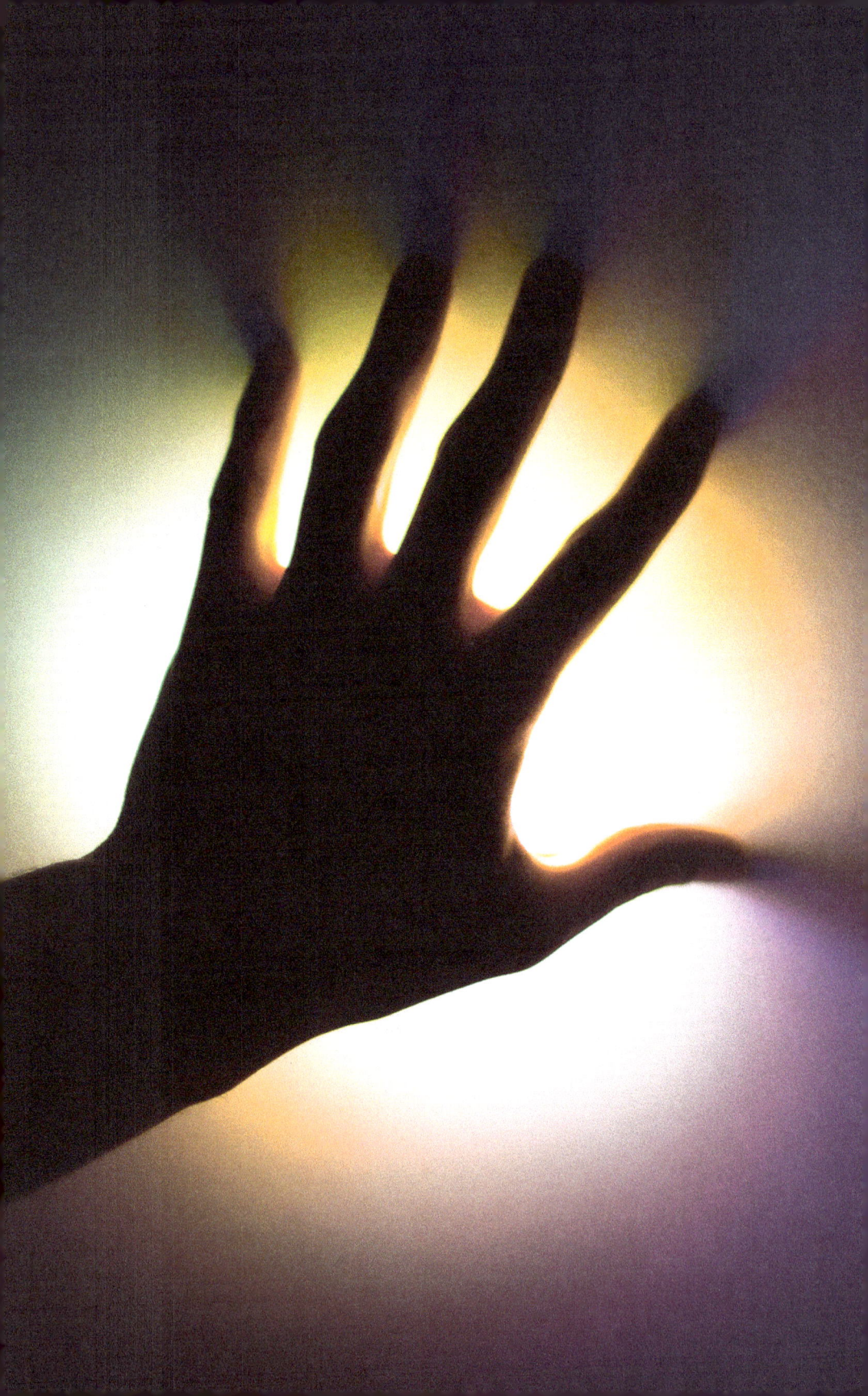

CHAPTER SIXTEEN

TWENY-SIX TRAITS THAT PUSH MEN AWAY AND HOW TO AVOID THEM

She showed up in my studio without an appointment.
 Her wedding had been canceled, and she was overwrought with grief. This was the third time this had happened. The first two men canceled on her at the last minute also. And now this! Kathleen couldn't understand why this kept happening to her. She had been a devoted lover and friend and given her all in each of her relationships. The wedding was one week away, and all the plans were in place. Family and friends had traveled from all over the world to attend the affair at the Beverly Hills Hotel.

We sat and talked. I let her tell me everything that she had been doing and what led to the ending of the relationship. Her fiancé, it had seemed to all of us, was head over heels in love with her. So this came as a shock.

It turned out the argument that ended the relationship was over a trivial matter, but the underlying issue was that Kathleen didn't feel the man was taking her opinions seriously enough. She felt that he always undermined her thoughts and ignored her feelings.

Oh, if only women understood and accepted, as well as appreciated, that men are logical beings whereas we are, for the most part, emotional beings, there would be less confusion and fewer misunderstandings. Most of the time, our responses are determined by how we're feeling on a particular day at that specific moment. What we like may shift from time to time. Men really can't figure us out because our behavior is just not logical to them. If and when they do get it right, then we think they love us. But when they get it wrong, then heaven forbid!

WHAT ARE YOU DOING TO REPEL MEN?

Are people happy when you walk into a room or overjoyed when you walk out? That is a good indicator of how you affect any relationship. Certain behaviors are an absolute no-no and will drive men away before you can say hello! If you've been looking for years for the right kind of man to share your life with and are frustrated, perhaps it's time to look at what it is that you are doing to repel men.

Perhaps it's not them but something about you that you need to change. Is it your approach, your attitude, what drives you, what you are inviting in, what and who you are tolerating and why? Is it the energy that you carry that isn't soft, isn't kind, isn't gentle—or perhaps it is one of desperation, anger, cynicism, bitterness?

If you wish to attract the man of your life then you must drop certain habits:

- Are you cold, needy, lazy, dishonest?
- Do you have anger issues; are you controlling, critical, a complainer?
- Do you constantly nag?
- Do you have a habit of disempowering men? By

cutting them off, by making fun of them, and dismissing their opinions?

- Are you a procrastinator?
- Do you constantly complain about life?
- Are you a man basher? Do you talk foul about your ex and your girlfriends?
- Do you come across as a victim in your life?
- Do you constantly put yourself down by being self-deprecating?
- Are you a woman in charge, or are you always humoring others?
- Are you one who sees problems all the time?
- Do you constantly project onto others that they are not enough?
- Do you come across as bored? Or are you a woman who is passionate about life?
- Do you lead with your resume, showing off and bragging about your successes and your accomplishments?

When you project onto others that they are not good enough, look at why you believe so. Is it because you feel *you* are not good enough? You must be willing to face your issues and complaints and deal with them, correct them, before you enter into a relationship. Are *you* willing to change?

Men are excited to be with a woman who lights up a room when she enters it, and they are turned on when they are with a woman who is passionate about life and living, who exudes inner confidence, who shows up relaxed because she knows her self-worth, who goes through life with a sense of purpose, who is gentle and kind and caring. They are looking for a woman who can bring more peace and joy into their lives, someone who is coming from a place of love and abundance, a woman who doesn't necessarily need him to fulfill anything for her but appreciates having him in her life.

Contrary to the belief that men are intimidated by a woman who is successful and in her personal power, in actual fact, most secure, conscious, masculine men are extremely attracted to that strength and empowerment. They are attracted to the woman who embraces who she is and recognizes her own value, who is self-aware but is at the same time also in her feminine power, not intimidating or standoffish. Ultimately, you have to allow and afford a man his place to show you that you are valuable to him by letting him be the man. Let him court you. It helps validate his worth as a man.

This doesn't mean that you have to water yourself down and play small just to appease him and make him love you, because if you do that, you're just setting yourself up for a false positive for him. You need not sacrifice your persona just to placate him. Stay true to yourself and be authentic in all ways while still affording him this place of trust. You're just creating the space for him to step in and serve you so that he feels wanted and trusted to provide and protect you. There is nothing more appealing and attractive to a man than to know that he is valued and that you believe in him and trust him.

WHAT WILL KEEP A MAN INTERESTED IN A WOMAN?

In preparing yourself to fully receive love, to keep a committed relationship with a conscious, healthy man, some effort is required on your part. In areas of your personality where you used to get it wrong, now you have the chance to get it right and be even more brilliant and attractive.

Expand your capacity to love. Be the person you wish to attract into your life. A man is not attracted to a woman who is waiting for him to complete her. He is attracted to a woman who is already that, who is already complete. Are you that person? Are you emitting that vibrational frequency that tells him that he belongs with you?

Awareness is the first and most crucial step in this process. Let's look at some areas that will help you keep your man interested in you:

1. **GET YOUR SEXY BACK!**

   Your appearance is the first thing that a man sees. Men are sexually attracted to a woman's physical magnetism. Your looks matter more than you think, and even though a man will love you for your sense of humor, your confidence, your caring attention, and your intelligence, how you package yourself—your hair, your clothes, your personal hygiene, and overall appearance—is what attracts him to you in the first place. Anything in your wardrobe that remotely whispers "frumpy" needs to be tossed out because how you look indicates how you feel. It's so easy to slack off in this area and stop taking care of yourself once you become comfortable and complacent in your relationship. Letting yourself go, packing on pounds, and slacking off on your hygiene and on how you dress are relationship killers. This lack of self-care is one of the reasons men tend to stray.

2. **STOP WHINING!**

   There's nothing worse than being with someone who is needy. Going into a relationship believing that your partner will complete you and solve all your problems is called *neediness*. He may be very much engaged in his work and easily neglect you, making you feel like he doesn't care or love you. You may resent him for his work and nag him, which is a huge turnoff. Stop asking or constantly calling to check if he needs anything, if he's okay, if he misses you (or to tell him that you miss him), monitoring his whereabouts, seeking his approval, or checking your e-mails and voicemails obsessively. A man can pick up your desperation and feel the constant pressure to be his very best, to be available and perfect to fit your image and expectations of him. He will pull away because of the responsibility he feels for your happiness. Besides, you are giving your power away and letting him know that you are at his mercy.

3. **TRASH YOUR "POOR ME" STORIES!**

   Refrain from bringing your past into your conversations. Speaking of your ex and your failed relationships, your parents and the injustices you may have experienced while growing up, and being catty and critical of your friends who may have done you wrong all take away from your irresistibility in his eyes. Tearing down others and elevating your worth generally backfires on you, because you are revealing an insecure and jealous side of your personality, which is not at all attractive to a man.

4. **LIGHTEN UP!**

   Humor and fun are a road map to your irresistibility. Amp up your charm, smile, and stop being a downer. Women who adopt a stern demeanor or are negative and constantly whine and incessantly complain show that they have lost their soft and girlish charm and instead have been hardened by their past. Sarcastic humor and a complaining attitude are a reflection of suppressed anger and a bitter outlook on life. Rather than playing the role of victim, be the star that you are and show off your gentle and warm personality. You are the leading lady in this game called love.

5. **NEVER REVEAL YOUR INSECURITIES!**

   Of course, there are times when we experience self-doubt and feel less than our very best. If you think a certain outfit doesn't make you look good then you're probably right, and you can correct it by looking through your wardrobe and changing into something else that makes you feel like a million dollars instead. Or, if you cannot help wondering whether you are lovable or attractive enough to your man, you should realize that he would not still be with you if he did not think so. There is no need to ask him these questions. Instead, show up in your full self-confidence and presence. Shake off these subpar thoughts, because nothing has meaning other than the meaning you give it. We tend to be our own worst critics.

6. STOP TALKING AND START LISTENING!

Have you ever been around a person who just won't shut up? It can be quite irritating. Chattiness and dominating the majority of your conversation is a terrible habit and can be quite annoying. Most women are guilty of this. Not really listening to your partner and instead drifting off into your thoughts and internal conversations, being distracted by what you want to say next, and preparing your response while he is still speaking are quite common traits. You only really hear what he is saying if it fits your agenda, and thus you are doing your relationship a great disservice. Trade off listening and talking in alternating turns so that you can get to know each other. Allow the other person to speak and hear what is being said; show interest and be attentive. This allows you to learn a few things about him and get to know him better. It also makes him feel he is special and that you care about his opinion, which makes *you* more attractive to *him*.

7. ENOUGH OF THE COMPARISON DIALOGUE!

One mistake many women make is talking about other men with the intention of inciting insecurity and jealousy. When you are with your current partner, leave other relationships, ex-boyfriends, ex-husbands, and ex-lovers out of the room. Leave the past in the past. Instigating competition and divulging past stories and relationships are insensitive and unkind behaviors and serve no purpose. And stop being condescending. It is a horrible habit and will alienate your partner.

8. STOP BEING SO SELF-ABSORBED!

Nothing turns men off more than a woman who is not able to receive love and deprioritizes relationships because she is solely focused on her career. Men are not attracted to women who are self-absorbed. It does not mean that you must dim down your intelligence and be less powerful. It just means that you may want to shift your focus and become more available and prioritize love and show the man that you are interested and really present in the relationship.

9. STOP EXCUSING BAD SEX!

Merely going through the motions just won't cut it. Sex between two consenting adults can be a beautiful and intimately bonding experience. It can be an excellent way to strengthen your feelings for each other and show that you care. However, culture and past conditioning can play quite a role in how we view sex and respond to intimacy in relationships. Perhaps you feel uncomfortable and shy about your body, thinking that you are not good enough. One of the causes of relationship breakups is complacent and boring sex. So be proactive; invest in sexy lingerie, initiate sex more frequently, and get in the mood to show your enjoyment and appreciation in each other rather than expecting your partner to do all the work. As with any aspect of a relationship, sex is about sharing, about giving and receiving pleasure and mutual satisfaction. To stand in your power and display your self-confidence and self-assurance about your body and show your man that you are irresistible and gorgeous just as you are is priceless. Enjoy revving up your sensual side!

10. INSINCERITY JUST WON'T WORK!

Your partner can sniff out any pretense fairly quickly. It's one thing to have an opinion or a perspective that is adverse to others' opinions, but to be fake and insincere when expressing it is a turnoff. Insincerity is an indication of insecurity and desperation in wanting others to like you. Worrying about what others think of your honesty and looking for their approval by going along is a shallow way of living. A healthy disagreement instead of an obnoxious and forceful opinion shows that you are sincere and comfortable about having a different perspective. It's much better to be kind and honest than to pretend to be what you are not. If that seems like you're not being honest then just try being neutral or not expressing an opinion at all.

11. STOP ALL THAT DISTRACTION!

In the fast-paced world we live in, there are many important things needing our attention. But if you have decided to spend some time together and are at a dinner or date or even a casual get-together, you must be fully present and put away your phones and tablets. Stop talking, texting, and e-mailing when you're in the company of others and when they're trying to have a conversation with you. It is an annoyance that can kill any relationship. Leave all your digital devices at home in favor of connecting and building the important relationship with your partner.

12. STOP PLAYING HARD TO GET!

Contrary to the advice offered by all the dating books of yesteryear, this is a tactic that will never produce a long-term and authentic relationship. It is a dishonest, manipulative, and scheming attempt to lure someone to like you but will only confuse him and turn him off after a while. He may play along for a brief period, but eventually it will get old and uninteresting, pushing him away to seek greener pastures. Men don't like complicated relationships.

13. RELINQUISH CONTROL!

There's nothing worse than letting a man know who is in charge. From the plans you make for outings, dinners, and vacations, to the decisions you "help" him make in his career and his life, even to implications that you know better than he does about what he should wear and how he should behave, these are all turnoffs, as most men do not appreciate being bossed around. Be gentle, and if you want to get your point across, you must do it in a way that makes him feel as if it were his idea and not yours.

14. STOP PLAYING THE BLAME GAME!

When something does not work for you, have a clear and honest dialogue with him. Let him know how you feel, and use the word "I" instead of "you." How you communicate means everything about your chances for your relationship's success or failure. Blaming a man for your bad feelings as if he were the one who caused them makes him defensive and resentful. You will lose his respect and immediately become unattractive to him to the point of no return.

15. STOP "MOTHERING" HIM!

Men are not attracted to women who behave like a mother to them. When you go overboard taking care of his feelings, you are actually emasculating him. It may endear you to him initially, but over time, all that caretaking may get annoying and he will be turned off. You cannot remain the object of his sexual affection for long if you continue to play that dominant role. He would rather you be a seductress than a mother in the relationship.

16. REMOVE "WE NEED TO TALK" FROM YOUR VOCABULARY!

These are words that make men cringe every time they hear them. It implies that something serious is at stake, that they will be accused of doing something wrong, or that you want to air some gossip or perhaps even grievances related to your relationship. The man's defenses go up immediately because no man wants to sit down and hear what he's done wrong nor does he want to listen at length to gossip. All men are interested in is "fixing" things. They're just not cut out for idle chitchat. Gossip and detailed conversation is what you share with your girlfriends.

17. ALLOW HIM TO BE THE MAN!

Men need to be needed. Let's face it: if you were absolutely perfect in every way, no man would be attracted to you because he will think that you don't need him. Men want to know that they can provide for you. They want to know that there is something they can do to make you happy. Let him take care of you. Let him open the door for you, take out the trash, fix the sink . . . You get the drift. Respecting the masculine energy he brings into your relationship and appreciating and acknowledging his efforts will make him want to do more for you. He will feel awesome and loved if he feels more like a man, like he is winning at taking care of you, and is valued while doing so.

18. LET HIM TRUST YOUR "NO" TO BELIEVE YOUR "YES"!

A masculine man is turned off by a "yes" woman because he feels she is too co-dependent, needy, guilt-inducing, and probably easily manipulated by any man. Make sure you uphold your self-worth and say no when it doesn't feel good or feel right, no matter the situation or who is asking. He will respect you when you stand up for your convictions, and you will have relayed a clear message that you can never be used by any man and that you are in control of your feelings and wants at all times.

19. RESPECT YOUR BODY!

Unless you are very sure he is the man you want in your life, hold off on having sex. A woman who gives her body to a man has a strong chance of feeling bonded to him even after only one good sexual encounter. Thus, it's very easy to bond with the wrong man. A man knows if he gets you to surrender, you're his with very little or no effort at all. By having casual sex, you're making it very clear to him that even though you don't know him well, you really don't care.

He can sense that your self-worth is shaky, and if he can get you to have sex with him with not much effort, then you must be just as easy and available with other men. A man who succumbs to lust alone has no reason to love. Wait until you know he loves you before he makes love to you. You're asking for committed sex and protecting yourself from being hurt and wasting your time if it is not leading anywhere. You are saving yourself from being confused and abused. However, once you are secure in feeling that you are good friends and you accept each other, imperfections and all, and that he is committed, then it is safe to consummate your relationship.

20. LEARN TO RECEIVE!

Stop over-giving, and learn to receive instead. This also pertains to any advice you are inclined to offer, because that is more giving. The more you treat yourself like a queen, the more your partner will step up to treat you like one as well. Men appreciate and respect women who practice self-care and who are not too easy to please. Rather than pursuing your partner and doing a guy's work, give a clear message that you appreciate and expect to be treated well, loved and cherished for who you are. And do this graciously and with gratitude. It's not by what you give, but by how you make him feel that you are valued.

21. BE AUTHENTIC!

Just as you want a man whose words and actions match, who is honest and has integrity, men want to be with a woman who is authentic. A woman who knows who she is and what she's looking for in her life—what her dreams are and what makes her happy—is a woman who is really confident and comfortable in her own skin. It inspires him to rise up and attempt to be that man who can provide all that for you. Share your passions, what lights you up. Be real. Be you.

22. STOP MANIPULATING!

If you come to the relationship with the condition that you will give to the man only when you get something in return from him then the relationship is doomed from the start. Men are really sensitive to manipulation, conniving, scheming, and strategizing. They shy away and will resent you for your controlling behavior. Also, stop justifying yourself or defending yourself. A relationship should not be about some kind of trade and exchange. It should be about honoring and respecting each other.

23. SWITCH YOUR PERSONA!

You can be a powerful, successful woman and make great money and your partner may not make as much. In a successful relationship, it's not about what he does, or how smart he is, where he came from, or even how successful he is. The only thing important is how he makes you feel about yourself, and if he makes you feel loved and seen, if he's devoted to you and adores you.

It's not that they are intimidated by your success, but what men are not attracted to is a woman who is in her head and behaves in a manly fashion, trying to boss them around, sparring with them, or debating with them. Rather than giving your opinion, switch to your feeling mode, and instead of using words like, "I think" choose instead to say, "I feel." Men like to feel heard. At work, you can show up in all your power, but switch into your soft, feminine mode when you're with him.

24. TREAD CAREFULLY IN SHARING YOUR OPINIONS!

Nothing turns off a man faster than a strong, independent, opinionated woman aggressively getting her point across. A man knows in minutes if the woman he is dating has potential by her behavior. There is a way to get your point across and still make him feel as if he is being included in the process. If you've decided on a major change in your life, such as selling or buying a house or a car, share these decisions by asking him for his input. You're not asking for his opinion, you're just letting him feel that he matters by displaying the possibility of a partnership.

25. STOP ALL THAT ADULT ATTACHMENT!

Men shy away from women who have the need to know where they are at all times. This need stems from insecurity and is like a radar system in your head, similar to a surveillance system that is operating all the time. You must have an idea where he is and that he's pretty much okay. Many men feel uncomfortable with too much closeness and intimacy and will find ways to keep you at arm's length, which in turn introduces a lot of doubt and insecurity into the relationship.

26. BE MINDFUL ABOUT NOT IMPLYING THAT HE CANNOT AFFORD YOU!

One of the things a woman is guilty of is flaunting what she has or what she is used to: the house, the car, the clothes she wears, her passion for travel and places she's been to, the lifestyle and luxury she may live in. She may do this either unconsciously because she has always lived this way or blatantly boast about it. When a man sees all that, he takes a step back and starts wondering how he can keep her happy. He assumes that everything she has is what she needs and decides he cannot offer her what she is used to. He wonders if she even needs him and comes to the conclusion that he really cannot afford her. Unknowingly, she has proven to him that she is not the right person. So he leaves. This is especially true in this day and age when so many women are outearning men.

Certainly you have much to offer a man. You're wonderful and all that, but if you're going about relationships the old way, and it's not working, isn't now the time to adopt new and improved mind-sets?

"When you seek love
with all your heart,
You shall find its echoes . . .
in the Universe."

—*Rumi*

PART IV

Getting to "I Do"

THE SOULMATE CHECKLIST

CHAPTER SEVENTEEN

IS HE HUSBAND MATERIAL?

*I*lene, thirty-two, is having trouble deciding if the guy she has been dating for three years is "The One." They've been engaged and broken up twice already, and now she's not so sure if she even wants to get married. She's afraid to commit lest the marriage ends in disaster. One thing she does know is that she loves him. But does he really love her enough to commit to a marriage that to her means "until death do us part"?

Ilene is not the only one who feels this way. Across the world, women are wondering what determines whether the guy they're dating is husband material.

Perhaps you can relate. You've been getting mixed signals from your boyfriend, and you're just not sure what his behavior is saying about your relationship. You're thoroughly confused because you think he really likes you, and you love him, too.

Sometimes, you wonder if you're dating a man or a boy. Even though your relationship is great, his controlling parents drive you crazy. He seems so attached to his family, and you feel as if you're an afterthought where they are concerned.

Then, there are times he shuts down and you are left wondering if it is something you said or did that has made him so moody and quiet. Of course, at times like this, it helps to know that men are made differently than women, and being talkative is not their forte. They say a woman speaks about eighty thousand words a day whereas a man speaks less than twenty thousand!

Even so, you had felt strongly that this relationship was meant to be but it is not working because something is wrong with you. So you resign yourself to the fact that you must not be destined to have love in your life and you're meant to be alone.

Sometimes, you end up giving so much more than you are receiving, and you do not feel you are being met halfway. You are confused and have this nagging suspicion you are not with someone who could be a full life partner, but yet you continue to try. Then you end up getting rejected, which is like adding insult to injury. You are heartbroken because you felt this deep soul connection to this person, and you hoped things would evolve and he would be "The One."

HOW DO YOU KNOW IF YOU'RE IN THE RIGHT RELATIONSHIP?

We want deep-lasting love and we yearn for a soul mate. We've spent way too much time investing in these relationships that seem to go nowhere. They start out so promising in the beginning, and we often find ourselves wondering, "Is this someone with real potential?"

So how do you know if you're in the right relationship or not? It's painful and confusing, especially when you've been in quite a few different relationships and experiences only to end up being alone again. You know well by now that it's not just chemistry that will carry a relationship.

The decision on whether or not to spend the rest of your life with a man is not to be taken lightly. It's a life-changing one and must be carefully made. How can you be certain he will be the person you can count on in sickness and in health, until death do you part?

Ask yourself, "If he never changes and remains exactly the same as he is now, would I still love him?" If you are not able to accept him as he is now before marriage, and you expect and believe you can fix him, or that he will change, then you are setting yourself up for disappointment.

Sometimes, the person you've been with seems so perfect, it feels just too good to be true. That can be a warning sign that you should slow down. It's not easy, because people can fake and pretend and put on their best behavior, and it can take months, sometimes years, for them to show their true colors. You can have amazing compatibility with someone and even be convinced he has potential, but if he can't be faithful, or he is an addict, or hypersensitive, or someone who is depressed, there is no future. The keys things to watch out for are:

- Does he handle stress well?
- When you disagree on something, how does he come across? Does he get angry and hostile?
- If you're busy and you have to say no to him, is he able to accept and respect your space?
- Does he have a habit of making mountains out of molehills?
- Does he become aggressive or shut down when something doesn't go according to his wishes?
- Is he aloof and self-absorbed?

- Is he the needy type who always wants you by his side and expects your constant attention on his needs?
- Is he good with time? Is he there when he says he will be?
- Are his place and surroundings clean and orderly?
- How does he treat his subordinates and service people?
- Is he able to contain himself, or does he yell and get mad at other drivers on the road or get frustrated when standing in line?
- Does he deny, dismiss, or discredit your opinions?
- Does he feel entitled?
- Does he make excuses and justifications for his behavior?
- Does he show displeasure at the way you dress, your posture?
- Does he make excuses, use others to back up his stories?
- Who is he with other people in his circle?
- Is he hot and cold, unsure and insecure?
- Is he moody?
- Is he too sensitive?

His behavior is a warning sign for you to be consciously aware of what's actually happening, to ask questions, to get to know him better before committing. Ask questions about his upbringing, his childhood, what his relationships with his siblings and his parents were like, and his relationships with his exes and children if he has any. If you pay close attention, you will realize that men tell the truth about who they are early on, but it's women who dismiss and think that they can change them.

I'm reminded of this quote by Maya Angelou: "When someone shows you who they are, believe them the first time."

You must remove your rose-colored glasses and see him clearly for who he is. You can't change people. It's not enough to have love nor is it enough to have chemistry. These alone cannot sustain a relationship when things go awry. The only option you have if you feel strongly about the relationship is to create an environment where he may be inspired to better himself. Ultimately, the choice is his. Whether he will evolve, become more conscious, grow, or change is his personal decision.

Ask yourself honestly, "Can this person be my life partner?"

HE IS "THE ONE" IF...

Assuming that you are also bringing your very best qualities to the relationship and pulling your weight in ensuring it is mutually fulfilling and healthy, then these signs will clearly tell you he is the one.

1. **HE EXCEEDS YOUR EXPECTATIONS.**

    Most couples become complacent and lazy in relationships. Does he go the extra mile to surprise and delight you? Is he your raving fan?

2. **HE RECOGNIZES YOUR NEEDS.**

    He is compassionate and caring and helps you feel safer and more secure in the relationship. He asks you what he needs to do or say so he can better understand your inner world and your love language. He meets your emotional needs and fosters a sense of intimacy, trust, and feeling of true love.

3. **HE MAKES YOU FEEL SPECIAL.**

    Being with him feels like you're on a constant date. He loves to make plans with you and goes out of the way to keep the spark and excitement alive. He verbalizes his appreciation for having you in his life and feels lucky to share his life with you. He compliments you and notices you. You are his priority.

4. **HE COMMUNICATES CLEARLY AND HONESTLY.**

   He is direct and honest in his communication with you. He is not afraid to have conversations and to talk things out, to face the truth so you can work things out when something is bothering either of you. He means what he says and does not play foolish games with your head and your heart. You can count on him not to lead you astray.

5. **HE REINFORCES HIS LOVE BY HIS LOVING DEEDS.**

   Mere words do not prove a person's love. The words "I love you" can be said a thousand times, but if the actions do not align with the words, then they are useless. His actions speak louder than his words, and everything he does shows you that he really loves and cares for you. Little things he performs each day prove that he's thinking of you and you are on his mind.

6. **HE RESPECTS YOUR FREEDOM.**

   Your free spirit is what attracted him to you in the first place, and he continues to respect that quality in you. At the same time, he appreciates the team spirit you share and reciprocates by never making you feel as if you are trapped in the relationship. He knows the relationship can only exist on the solid foundation of trust and teamwork that comes from a healthy dose of freedom.

7. **HE EMBRACES YOUR PERSONAL GROWTH.**

   As you both evolve, he is there to celebrate and share in your personal growth and connects with you from a deep and loving place. He appreciates how you love spending time together and nurture each other on your journey together. Instead of constantly expecting give and take, you have chosen to share each other's joy and pain and to experience life together through good and not-so-good times. You know you can lean on him just as you are there for him to lean on.

8. HE DOES NOT ALLOW OUTSIDERS TO INFLUENCE HIS RELATIONSHIP WITH YOU.

Your journey together is yours to travel together, and any personal issues you have are private matters. He does not involve or allow outsiders such as family and friends to influence his decisions. He cares and respects you and would rather work things out in the privacy of your own relationship.

9. HE COMPLIMENTS YOU EVEN ON YOUR WORST DAYS.

He tells you how beautiful you are and makes you feel special even on days when you are not feeling and looking your best. In his eyes, you are the most beautiful thing that ever happened to him.

10. HE ENJOYS SHARING HIS DAYS WITH YOU.

It gives him joy to hear how your day went, and he loves to share interesting stories or challenges of his own days as well. He loves the daily interactions and makes sure to let you know that you are a bigger part of his life.

11. HE INVOLVES YOU IN HIS DECISIONS.

He includes you and shares in the decision-making process and values your opinion and input. He wants to make sure you understand how important you are in his present and future plans.

12. HE ENJOYS SPENDING TIME WITH YOU.

You never have to ask him to spend time with you, because nothing gives him more pleasure. At the same time, he is sensitive when you need your space and gives you that freedom while letting you know that he is always there for you should you need him.

13. HE TREATS YOU WITH RESPECT WHEN IN THE COMPANY OF OTHERS.

He enjoys letting others know how precious you are to him and includes you in his interactions and conversations with others. Because he shows you respect, he expects others to afford the same courtesy to you.

14. HE IS YOUR BIGGEST FAN.

You know he's always there to cheer you on and celebrate your victories. He always encourages you to be better than your best. He is not intimidated by your money and your success but rather feels proud of you.

15. HE MAKES PROMISES AND KEEPS THEM.

You can always count on him to follow up on his promises. He does not make promises he cannot keep, and you respect that about him and trust him not to disappoint you.

16. HE MAKES YOU FEEL SEXY AND WANTED.

You are best friends, partners, and confidants. But above all, he makes you feel like a woman and communicates clearly how much he desires you and that you are his woman. He makes you feel sexy and very much loved. He compliments you every chance he gets so you know how special you are to him.

17. HE MAKES YOU FEEL SAFE.

You know that he will always be there to protect you, and regardless of his size and stature, he would take a bullet for you if push came to shove. He will never allow anyone to abuse you or hurt or harass you in any way. You can relax and allow yourself to be cared for and nurtured. You feel safe with him. He is one person you can count on for richer or for poorer, in sickness and in health.

18. HE IS FINANCIALLY SOUND.

He has a good job and a solid work history. He is a hard worker and takes pride in his vocation. He is financially stable and prepared to take care of you and your children and wishes to do so willingly and gladly.

19. HE IS GENEROUS.

He always wants you to have more than he does and will gladly give you the bigger closet, the bigger portion of food, and the better part of anything and everything in his life. He is generous with his money and his time, and you love his acts of selflessness.

20. HE HAS AN EASY AND FORGIVING ATTITUDE.

He does not get upset when you or your children spill food and drinks on the carpet or in his car. He is not fussy about messy children, doesn't faint at the sight of diapers, and shows lightheartedness when dealing with these or any other stressful situations.

21. HE IS COURTEOUS AND RESPECTFUL OF YOUR FAMILY.

He gladly accompanies you to visit your parents and engages in enthusiastic conversations and gets involved in your family gatherings as part of the family. He knows how important they are to you and cares for your happiness.

22. **HE RESPECTS AND GETS ALONG WELL WITH HIS FAMILY.**

    He's kind to his parents and checks in with them often, but not in an obsessive manner. He loves his siblings and helps them when they are in need. His nieces and nephews are close to him and like to spend time with him.

23. **HE WOULD MAKE A WONDERFUL FATHER.**

    He tells you he likes children and would like to have one with you someday. He expresses interest in meeting your children and shows up with gifts for them and wins their hearts. He even plans dates where they are included, and let's them see how much he cares and respects you. He cares for your children and encourages them to do well in school and is a sound influence in their lives.

24. **HE REALLY SEES YOU.**

    How he interacts with you warms your heart. You know that you have his undivided attention whenever you say anything. He listens deeply and is fully present with you. He looks at you when you speak, and you know that he cares. He really gets you and sees you for the person you are.

25. **HE GOES ALONG WITH ANYTHING AND EVERYTHING THAT MAKES YOU HAPPY.**

    He indulges your guilty pleasures. He will go out of the way to bring home your favorite dessert, sit through your favorite girly movies, and indulge you when you want to shop. He does all of these with love and is happy just to see you happy.

26. HE HAS A GOOD SENSE OF HUMOR.

Life can be serious at times. When you are with him, you know that he will always cheer you up and make you smile. He is never condescending and never makes fun of your fears. Any fears or concerns that you may have evaporate because he is there to help you lighten up and kiss them away.

27. HE IS CAPABLE OF FORGIVENESS.

He does not hold a grudge when you do something that may seem unforgivable or questionable. He loves you enough to want to talk and work things out gently and without judgment.

28. HE IS HYGIENIC AND WELL GROOMED.

You notice how impeccably he dresses and that he maintains his hygiene to a fault. He keeps his house clean and organized and even knows how to cook a few decent meals. He takes pride in his environment and is mindful about littering in public places. His car is always clean and the gas tank full.

29. HE IS RESPECTFUL OF THE BOUNDARIES YOU SET.

You have certain expectations of your man, and you let him know up-front what they are and what you want out of your union. You make it clear the kind of relationship you want; you expect him to be faithful and monogamous, responsible and family-oriented, and you make it clear you expect to be treated like a lady. Your needs and wants are clearly spelled out, and he knows he wants to see you happy. He respects you and makes sure he delivers.

30. HE APPRECIATES YOU.

> He appreciates having you in his life and shows it. Your involvement in all decision-making, your opinions and decisions in handling finances and the running of the household are all well acknowledged and appreciated by him.

In an age of easy divorces, it is easy to become skeptical of marriage. Our expectations are inflated, and we want a guarantee that the person we marry is so amazing and perfect that we will be absolutely sure it will last a lifetime.

For a marriage to last, both spouses have to work at it, constantly and consistently. Appreciating your partner, not undermining his confidence, and communicating your needs and wants clearly are some of the best attitudes you can adopt for a long-lasting relationship.

Just as you have imperfections, no man is 100 percent perfect. But there is a man who is perfect for *you*. If you have such a man in your life, you are very lucky indeed. You have found a person who will treat you the way you truly deserve. He is certainly husband material.

On the other hand, until you feel certain he is the one for you, it's better to live alone with dignity than commit to a relationship that will never meet your needs, that demands you sacrifice your happiness and self-respect.

Value your true self and love your true life. Happiness is ultimately your responsibility and can only arise from the love you find within.

"Give your hearts, but not into each other's keeping.

For only the hand of Life can contain your hearts.

And stand together, yet not too near together:

For the pillars of the temple stand apart,

And the oak tree and the cypress grow not in each other's shadow."

—Kahlil Gibran

CHAPTER EIGHTEEN

ASK THOSE QUESTIONS NOW!

*T*ying the knot with someone you love is one of the happiest moments of your life.

You have finally met the man of your dreams who is living a lifestyle that fits right in with the life you visualized for yourself. He has everything you've always wanted: killer looks, money, fame, and a wonderful reputation to boot. When he kneels down on his knees and asks you to be his wife, *of course* you accept!

WHAT DO YOU REALLY KNOW ABOUT HIM?

But how much do you know about the man you have promised to spend the rest of your life with? Have you considered all the ups and downs that are a part of a life together, the good times and the not-so-good ones, and the other relationships that will be woven into the thread of you as a couple? Can you confidently say that you can weather any storms that may blow your way until death do you part?

It is true that we are very good at planning a wedding but have no clue about planning a marriage. Knowing that you both are truly committed to each other takes many heart-to-heart conversations that preferably take place before you say, "I do."

Ideas around money, blending families, and religious or spiritual considerations can all be sticky subjects for couples. Successful marriages are often the product of healthy premarital decisions and a willingness to work on the relationship before saying "I do."

Knowing the answers to questions that cover different areas of your lives, alone and together as partners in marriage, is the key to a successful, healthy, happy, and lasting relationship. Begin by asking the man to be up-front with you about what he wants out of your relationship and how he sees your future together. Make sure he is saying what he wants and you're making clear what you don't want. Be honest with each other. If the answers are not forthcoming, and you are not yet on a sure footing with him, then just be patient and, in the process, stay anchored in your self-love.

Women are afraid to ask these questions because they think they will scare their partner away. You must get over the fear of losing your man and confront him instead of remaining in the dark, not knowing the answers to your questions and always second-guessing yourself. Even more important is to be honest when asking brutally candid questions as well as to be forthcoming with equally honest answers.

If your partner does not like what you propose then be open to hearing him out and willing to negotiate. Intimidating him with logical arguments and expecting him to compromise in any way may solve your short-term goal but will not serve either of you in the long haul. All you're doing is asking him to serve your feelings before he asks you to serve his thinking. Always negotiate for your mutual benefit.

If the answers you receive are uncomfortable, then at least you know you need more time until you feel confident about committing to the relationship. However, if over time you still do not become more comfortable with his answers, then leaving the relationship is a risk that may be worth taking.

After all, you don't want to become just another statistic, do you? The divorce rate today is 50 percent for first marriages, 64 percent for second marriages, and a staggering 73 percent for third marriages. So, it behooves you to ask yourself the following questions and honestly look at what comes up:

1. **DO YOU LOVE HIM JUST AS HE IS?**

    What you may find irritating about him now may continue to grate on you after you're married. Don't kid yourself into thinking that he will change. Be prepared to live with any flaws you see, any negative qualities he exudes, and decide if these are deal breakers for you now, before it's too late.

2. **DO YOU KNOW HIS FINANCIAL SITUATION?**

    Aside from what he makes from his salary, find out about his savings and any debt he may be carrying, and most important, how he accrued those debts. It will give you a clear indication of his spending and saving patterns. It also allows you both to plan for future financial emergencies.

3. **DO YOU BOTH WANT CHILDREN?**

    What are your views on growing your family? If you want children but he doesn't, are you willing to compromise? If you both agree on either wanting or not wanting children, it will save you from future stress, knowing you are on the same page. You are being honest about how you feel. This subject is vital in your decision-making; otherwise, you may grow to resent each other for the rest of your lives together.

4. **WHAT TURNS YOU BOTH ON IN BED?**

    They say sex is the glue that holds a relationship together. Knowing that you will not just be roommates but have a fulfilling sex life is important. If you are not attracted to each other sexually, there is a chance that either or both of you may seek fulfillment elsewhere after you are married. By having this discussion, you are addressing sexual intimacy issues and working toward solutions that will contribute to mutual satisfaction and happiness.

5. **CAN HE HELP FIX THINGS AROUND THE HOUSE IF NECESSARY?**

    Having a basic knowledge about the tools in a toolbox and being able to change bulbs and doorknobs or hang a picture means that you don't have to factor those expenses into the basic needs of everyday living and will keep you from nagging him when you want something done.

6. **DO EITHER OR BOTH OF YOU KNOW HOW TO COOK?**

    You don't need to be a chef. But knowing basic things, such as making coffee and preparing simple home-cooked meals, will save you money as well as keep you from eating unhealthy, microwave-ready prepackaged foods. Being able to feed yourselves is an important life skill. Besides, the way to a man's heart is through his stomach. . . .

7. **IS HE GENEROUS?**

    A man who cherishes you will like giving more to you and being generous with you. The feeling that you "need" him will make him feel wanted and secure in your love. As a result, he will want to protect you and take care of you, and in return, you will feel secure and respect him for the love you share. Nourishing a man's self-esteem and allowing him to take care of you does not mean that you are submissive or "less than." On the contrary: it means that you value and appreciate him in your life.

8. **HOW WILL YOU HANDLE EXPENSES?**

    Is he frugal with money? Do you know how he would spend a large sum of money if it were made available to him? Would he blow it rather than pay off his debts? This will give you a clear indication of his spending patterns, his money risk, and tolerance level. Knowing how to protect your personal assets and deciding how you will be taking care of joint expenses is crucial. Many marriages suffer because couples have not made it clear how they will handle money issues. A "yours, mine, and ours" approach may be best. Set up and agree on a checking/savings account that will be used to pay household expenses and groceries, as well as big purchases such as travel and vacations. And at the same time, set boundaries on what each can spend with their own hard-earned money. This will help in the long run.

9. **SIGNING A PRENUPTIAL AGREEMENT.**

    When one is in love, this can be overlooked. However, since so many marriages end in separation or divorce today, having a prenuptial agreement in place is wise. It helps each partner keep what was originally his or hers in individual, separate accounts. This saves you from being embroiled in any lawsuits or being held accountable for your spouse's previous debts so that you don't risk having to split your premarital assets in a divorce.

10. KEEP YOUR NAME OR CHANGE IT?

Of the various options you have, which one would you want to reflect your new identity after marriage? You can either keep the one you have now, take a hyphenated name, or combine your names into one new one. Determine what feels right to you and what is important to both of you.

11. MORTGAGE: A MUTUAL DEBT.

If purchasing a house is one of the more important things on your list, then be aware that this major purchase is a debt that you will both be taking on as a couple. Unless you have a home that is under the prenup agreement, then it does not matter whose name your property is in; you are both liable for the joint mortgage if you split up.

12. TALK ABOUT YOUR PAST RELATIONSHIPS.

It is only fair to ask him why his previous relationship didn't work out. Does he have a history of unfaithfulness? Does he have a history of being an abuser or of being abused? If you pay attention to how he talks about his exes, it will give you an insight into his personality. Why did he split up? Was he unfaithful? Consumed by his work? Or was he overly possessive? The way he talks about past events, or if he's defensive and territorial and blames the other persons, may not be a good sign. If, however, he takes responsibility for the bad choices he may have made, then that's a good indication of his maturity and that he likes and respects the women in his life and that he has nothing to hide from you.

13. YOUR FUTURE TOGETHER AND HOW YOU SEE IT IN FIVE, TEN, TWENTY YEARS, AND BEYOND.

It's important to know what is important to both of you and discuss what your dreams and goals are. What are your short-term goals? And how about your long-term goals? Do you have a plan in place? Your goals may be about setting up your own business, having children, or purchasing a home. It's not that you need to plan out your entire life, but you should have a road map to ensure that you each have a vision and you don't get so entangled in your partner's goals and dreams that you forget what yours were. Compromising on your goals can make you unhappy and cause your marriage to suffer in the long run.

14. ADDICTIONS, IF ANY?

It could be that your partner loves drinking. That's harmless on the face of it. However, if you have seen that he drinks every day and goes through at least one bottle alone in one sitting, then that may be a cause of concern. Or does he do drugs? Watch pornography? These are red flags that need to be addressed so that they don't spiral out of control after you are married.

15. RELIGIOUS OR SPIRITUAL PREFERENCE?

Do you have the same faith or believe in the same religion? If not, is he fine with giving you freedom to practice your own faith? What about children? If and when you have any, which religion will they be expected to adopt? Or if you are not religious but spiritual instead, will he expect you to attend church with him, practice his faith? Is religion more important to him than your relationship? You certainly do not want to marry a religious fanatic.

16. ARE YOU BOTH READY FOR UNCONDITIONAL COMMITMENT?

This is a question that is very timely in today's atmosphere of rampant infidelity. Do you both believe in monogamy, and are you committed to each other even if and when either feels attracted to another person? Are you committed to each other through sickness and in health? Does your partner shy away from illness of any kind?

17. HOW DO YOU FEEL ABOUT THERAPY?

If push came to shove, and your relationship suffered major misunderstandings, would you both be open to marriage counseling and therapy? Would you be open to bringing in outside help for the two of you in the hope of finding resolution and getting your marriage back on healthy ground?

18. HOW WILL YOU BE TAKING CARE OF YOUR PARENTS?

Although this is a difficult subject to discuss or even think about, your parents will age, and how you will help and care for them should be taken into consideration. Are you in line to be the de facto caregiver for your not-so-friendly mother-in-law? Will you need to install some bars in your bathtub or rack up frequent-flyer miles to make sure your parents are being properly cared for? Or are you headed toward an argument about the merits of nursing care? So that you have a smooth road ahead, it is best to put a plan in place now.

19. WHAT DO YOU FIND BORING ABOUT YOUR LIVES?

Have your weekends become a tedious affair of other not-so-fun agendas such as lawn care, neighborhood obligations, children's birthday parties, and family visits? Are you or he bored in bed? Of eating the same meals day in and day out?

20. **WHAT'S THE ONE THING YOU WISH EACH WOULD STOP DOING?**

There are ways that each of you might be annoying your partner—little habits such as leaving dirty laundry on the bathroom floor, not putting down the toilet seat, leaving used tea bags on the kitchen counter, and so on. The list could be endless. Perhaps you could each agree on one tiny, weekly change that could relieve some pressure and show that you're willing to try and cooperate just to see each other happy.

21. **HOW WILL YOU HANDLE QUARRELS?**

Arguments in any relationship are inevitable. How will you manage conflict? How you handle fights and whatever your argument style is, hash out what counts as acceptable behavior and what behavior is off-limits. In a healthy relationship, each must accommodate the other and try not to let ill feelings fester for long. Refusing to talk it out is the death of a relationship. Giving each other the silent treatment is a no-no.

22. **AGREE TO DISAGREE ON HOBBIES AND PASTIMES.**

Let him know of your passions and ask him about his. You may like to have personal time to go shopping, go for a massage, or be alone on the beach occasionally. He may be into golf, working on his car, or watching football. Make sure you understand what makes each of you happy and agree to give each other room to have personal time.

23. WHAT ARE YOUR DEAL BREAKERS?

It's never too early to let your partner know what, if anything, will drive you nuts in the marriage. For example, you will not be able to tolerate flirtatious behavior toward other women or gambling away your mutual savings at roulette. It is best to talk it out sooner rather than later.

24. HAVE YOU NEGOTIATED?

Most likely, you both have careers that are important to you and would like to be intimate after work. Negotiate how you will each share your home and family responsibilities, where you will live, who will handle the money, investments, and bill paying, and be clear about commitment boundaries so that there is no discord later.

25. YOUR BUCKET LISTS.

What are your life goals and your dreams? Make sure he is open to supporting you in fulfilling them. You may wish to own your own home someday, travel, and explore other continents, or even aim to live in another country or own your own business. Ask him about his bucket list and support him in his quest.

26. ALLOCATING TIME.

How do you allocate "my," "your," and "our" time? Are you getting a day to spend with your family and friends, and does he get a day to spend with his? Which day of the week will you spend away from each other? What about vacation time, and when can you both take them together? Or do you take long vacations away from each other with your families? What about annual celebrations such as Christmas and New Year's, Easter and

Thanksgiving? How do you decide where and with whom these will be spent?

27. ALLOCATING ACTIVITIES.

Which activities do you want to do together? What about the ones you want to do without him? And how about the ones you want to do separately with others? Make clear requests and come to mutual agreements that satisfy both of you.

28. THE LITTLE DAILY HABITS.

A long and formal courtship before saying "I do" allows you to share meaningful moments together so that you can see his attitudes and responses when faced with a variety of circumstances and challenges in life such as the following:

- How does he react when experiencing anger, frustration, or a stressful situation?
- How does he react when he is faced with a problem or when he is feeling sad?
- How does he act when he is around your or his family members and friends?
- Is he supportive of you when you need him, or does he shy away and abandon you?
- Is he a hardworking and responsible being?
- Is he jealous or controlling?
- What about his personal care and hygiene? What are his living habits?
- How is he around children?

You need to uncover all the little habits and figure out if they are acceptable to you so that you can make an educated decision about your future together. Actions do speak louder than words.

29. WHAT ARE HIS POLITICAL VIEWS?

For many, this is a taboo topic. Does he take interest in politics or his country? Is he inclined toward supporting other nationalities, countries, and their causes? If so, is he fanatic about it? Can you deal with this attitude for the long haul?

30. HOW DOES HE BEHAVE WHEN FACED WITH ILLNESS?

Sickness can be depression, a common cold, a complicated pregnancy, or at the worst, battling terminal cancer. It can be mental, emotional, or spiritual as well. Men are known to act like big babies when faced with the faintest hint of an illness. They require attention. How does he react when he sees you not feeling well? Does he comfort you, go out of his way to make sure you have all the medicines you need, provide you with all the comforts that will help make you better? And does he compliment you and let you know how beautiful you still are to him no matter what your condition?

31. HOW DOES HE TREAT YOU IF AND WHEN YOU MAKE A MISTAKE?

Is he understanding and compassionate? True love keeps no record of wrong. The supreme test of true love is to forgive each other. You may have disappointed or hurt your partner, in which case it is healthy to articulate and talk things out. Be angry if you must, but get over it and don't hold it against each other. Try to quell things before they escalate to a point of no return. Every relationship experiences times when one does something that is not to the other's liking. Things that he said and you said can be quite hurtful, but being able to forgive each other and move on is the only solution for a successful marriage.

32. DOES HE HAVE UNFAIR EXPECTATIONS OF YOU?

Does he see your inner beauty, or is he merely in love with your looks and what you bring to the relationship? Does he expect you to behave a certain way that is adverse to your true nature? Having to be constantly on guard in trying to be perfect in another's eyes at all times can be exhausting and chips away at your inner happiness and joy. Accepting each other's inevitable imperfections and letting go of the expectation of perfection is the kindest thing one can do in a relationship.

33. HOW MATURE IS HE IN HIS BEHAVIOR, HIS OUTLOOK?

It is common knowledge that men mature later in life than women. Is he still behaving like a boy, always wanting his own way? Is he mature enough to handle life situations with grace and understanding? Does he possess selfishness, bitterness, and jealousy? Is he petty? No one is perfect, but how he handles any situation is how he will handle your relationship.

34. WHEN HE MAKES DECISIONS, ARE THEY MADE OUT OF FEAR?

Career choices, life circumstances, and any small and large decisions that he makes: are they made with good and sound intentions, or are they made out of haste and out of fear? Is he marrying you because he is afraid to lose you or to be without you, and vice versa? During your years together, you will face situations that may be terrifying and complicated. You want to make sure that the person you are marrying is someone you can depend on to come through every challenge with a strong heart and mind.

35. HOW DOES HE HANDLE CONFLICT?

Conflict is certain in all marriages. However, it does not have to be negative to the point of creating bitterness and resentment. Does he show uncontrollable anger, stonewalling, and even violence? If you find that he gets angry easily and often while you're dating then that trait may get a lot worse once you are married. Learning to resolve conflict can have many positive benefits, provided it is handled in a positive way. Healthy conflict and its resolution allows for intimacy and understanding.

36. IS HE A HUMBLE PERSON?

Or does he think he is a perfect human being who can do no wrong? The worst thing you can do is marry a person who isn't perfect but who thinks he is. People without humility typically spend all their energy defending themselves rather than evaluating their actions and correcting their behaviors. You must ask yourself if this man ever serves others, or does he insist on being served all the time? Does he take any initiative in caring for another, or is he obsessed with how he is treated and appreciated? Does he show empathy toward the feelings of another, or is he always trying to impress and prove how wonderful he is?

37. IS HE A TAKER?

Some people are givers, and some only know how to take. Even though you may be a giver and find joy in giving all the time, there will be times when you will need to receive as well. Ask yourself if your partner can learn how to give. Sadly, a taker does not ever know what it is to give. Marriage is a long journey, and this is one area that you must weigh carefully. Do you feel drained or invigorated when you are around him? How would you describe your relationship: healing and supportive, or exhausting and combative? The answer will set you free.

38. HOW IS HIS RELATIONSHIP WITH HIS FAMILY?

How does he feel about his mother? His father? If he had a good relationship with his parents, he was raised with a core set of values, which is a good indication of the values he will bring to your home. Likewise, how he treats his mother and sisters shows the respect he will afford you in the relationship.

Of course, with age and experience, your needs and interests and goals may change over time. What you look for and want ten or twenty years after marriage will probably be quite different from what you had decided when you were just starting out. That does not mean that you are weak; it just means that you have evolved and are open to new ideas and experiences and are flexible enough to go for what you feel is best for both of you later in life.

Life has a tendency to throw us curveballs, and even the best-laid plans can change. Through all the ups and downs, never stop working on your own spiritual, physical, mental, and emotional health, as that is the best gift you can give to your partner. Your well-being is the key to the stability and health of your relationship.

Couples with the most flexibility and ability to adapt to change are the ones whose relationships will last beyond the norm. This is what contributes to a healthy marriage.

Couples who refuse to discuss or ignore red flags in the relationship, expecting them to go away, are headed toward a journey of disaster. Marriage will only get more complicated if you have not walked through all these issues beforehand.

Ask yourself: Are you honestly willing to look at your own shortcomings? Are you ruthlessly honest about your own "brokenness"? Trying to change your partner may seem like a noble pursuit, but ultimately the only person you can change is *you*.

Continue to ask and you will receive the answers.

You are the lock and you are the key.

"The breeze at dawn
has secrets to tell you.

Don't go back to sleep.
You must ask for
what you really want.

Don't go back to sleep.
People are going back and forth
across the doorsill

Where the two worlds touch.
The door is round and open.
Don't go back to sleep."

—*Rumi*

CHAPTER NINETEEN

NEVER TAKE EACH OTHER FOR GRANTED

"Long-term relationships, the ones that matter, are all about weathering the peaks and the valleys."

—Nicholas Sparks

*L*ove is not perfect. You are here to learn and grow with each other, supporting each other along the way. There will be times where you're expressive and times when you're explosive; you will love large and perhaps fall as heavily. It is what goes into a shared life and a "big love."

Each of us yearns to be loved fully, completely, and unconditionally. Yet we ourselves have not opened up our hearts to create a space of generosity and acceptance and unconditional love for others. We have not even learned to love our own selves in that way, constantly wondering if we're good enough, or worthy enough, to even be loved.

A few years into a relationship, most couples tend to become complacent and to take each other for granted. Both people in the relationship get sloppy in the way they present themselves to each other, and keeping the romance alive seems to be too much effort.

Not so this couple . . .

Phyllis and Jean Paul have been married for fifteen years, and not a day goes by that he does not bring her flowers or surprise her with a little gift just to see the light in her eyes. It makes his day, and she in turn sends adoration his way in the form of a hidden love note in his trouser pocket or loving messages all day long to let him know she is thinking of him.

If you can relate to Phyllis and Jean Paul, then you are very lucky indeed. The challenging world of marriage with all its ups and downs is fraught with complaints from those in relationships struggling to keep their family nucleus intact.

It is a proven fact that what we do for each other *before* marriage is *not* an indication of how we will conduct ourselves *after* marriage. We tend to revert to being the people we were before we "fell in love," and our true personalities are revealed as we grow complacent and settle into our relationship.

Priorities become somewhat misplaced. For most men and women today, work comes first, and love is way down their lists. It is no wonder, then, that love doesn't work. We take each other for granted and therein lies the downfall of most marriages.

Building a healthy, lasting relationship takes presence and focus and mutual care and attention. It is not only about loving or serving the other person; it's about loving who you are together.

There are tremendous benefits to meeting the emotional needs of your partner, of course, but not at the expense of ignoring your own emotional needs. A relationship between two people can be no healthier than the emotional health of the least-healthy person. Thus, when two healthy individuals invest their energy to build a wonderful life together, life becomes beautiful.

AVOID THESE PITFALLS

Below is a list of some of the pitfalls couples must avoid if they want to grow their relationship:

1. **FEELING TOO RUSHED TO COMMUNICATE.**

   Be present. The moments spent with your partner in "total awareness," by cultivating deep listening and being fully present, are the best gifts you can give. Simply listen patiently without judging. Let your partner draw you into the conversation and connect deeply. Let him see that you value him; allow him to see his beauty through your eyes. Let your partner know you value his presence in your life.

2. **NOT PAYING COMPLIMENTS BECAUSE YOU ARE TOO COMFORTABLE WITH EACH OTHER.**

   Expressing a kind word, a smile, complimenting your partner on his attire, or even acknowledging his accomplishments goes a long way in showing him how much you appreciate and love him. One habit that you can adopt is ending each day by sharing three things you appreciate that your partner did that day. When you show appreciation, you show how much you value him.

3. **NOT SHOWING GRATITUDE.**

   When you're on a date, make sure you thank him. It could be for the restaurant he chose, the meal he paid for, or the wonderful time you had. Men love words of affirmation as much as women do. They want to know that they provided you with a good time and were good company. Be effusive in your gratitude. Be genuine in thanking him. It will make him feel secure and appreciated, and ideally he's going to get back in touch with you about scheduling another date.

4. **CONSTANTLY TRYING TO "FIX" YOUR PARTNER.**

   No one is perfect. Being in a relationship with another is a choice you make whereby you love the person just as he is. Imperfection is rampant in each of us, but by trying to "fix" your partner, you are just pushing him away and making him withdraw so he is afraid to share himself, his ideas, and his thoughts with you. Caring for another must be rooted in love and respect and in allowing him to be himself.

5. **INTERFERING WITH EACH OTHER'S GROWTH.**

   It is to be expected that you keep growing and changing as your relationship evolves. In a healthy relationship, each partner needs to give the other room to grow and allow him or her to feel comfortable in the process. Impeding his growth and wanting him to remain the same and insisting he humor you by restricting the process to suit your comfort level will just push him away.

6. **KEEPING SECRETS FROM EACH OTHER.**

   Honesty and trust are the pillars of a long-lasting relationship. Omissions are just as bad as telling lies. The truth invariably will be revealed at some time or the other, and your relationship may then reach a point of no return and be ruined forever. At that point, it may be impossible to repair and heal. Speaking the truth, no matter what the consequence, contributes to a peaceful relationship. Everyone has problems and faults, but trying to hide them does not allow another to truly know and love you.

7. **LETTING FEAR OVERPOWER YOUR LOVE AND TRUST.**

   Holding back for fear that another may judge you and not love you is akin to lacking trust in your love for each other. Love means giving another the power to hurt you but trusting he or she won't because you have faith in the relationship. A relationship cannot survive without trust.

8. **FOCUSING ON THE PAST AND HOLDING ON TO PAST GRUDGES.**

   Let go of the past, make peace with it, and stop allowing it to affect your present. There is nothing to be gained by bringing it up and reliving it. Regroup, make amends if you must, and forgive if you can. Either way, just move on.

9. **EXPECTING YOUR PARTNER TO VALIDATE YOUR IDENTITY.**

   Be yourself at all times. Waiting for another to like you, to validate you, verifies your insecurity about yourself. Work on loving and respecting yourself more by being mindful of your inner self-talk. Be with someone who celebrates you rather than just tolerates you.

10. **EXPECTING YOUR PARTNER TO BE STRONG AND TO TAKE CARE OF YOU.**

    Everyone has his struggles and challenges. Your partner may not always have the strength to hold you up, but it does not mean that he does not love you. In a healthy relationship, it is not fair to expect another to fill your empty inner space. You are responsible for your problems in dealing with your pain, emptiness, and boredom that you may experience at certain times in your life together.

11. GIVING OUT OF OBLIGATION AND EXPECTING TO BE COMPENSATED IN RETURN.

Doing something for another only for the sake of it being reciprocated is not true love. You do it because it makes you happy and because you appreciate the joy it brings to another. Instead of wondering what's in it for you, ask, "How may I serve and what can I give?" The rewards you will reap will far surpass the act you perform.

12. FAKING YOUR FEELINGS.

Be yourself in all ways—always. Pretending to be someone you are not is rarely sustainable, and it can become restrictive and draining. Be real and authentic. Be you.

13. HOLDING YOUR PARTNER RESPONSIBLE FOR YOUR HAPPINESS.

Happiness is every individual's own responsibility. Holding your partner responsible for your state of being is not fair to him. When you're happy, you give that energy to your partner and allow him to be happy, too. But you have to be receptive to happiness and be willing to allow your partner to make you happy instead of shutting down. The only way you can do so is to relinquish control and "allow." Be rested and put in the time and energy for self-care so that you are restored and open to receiving.

14. TALKING MORE THAN LISTENING.

Opening up one's mind and heart to deeply listen is an art in itself. Rather than doing all the talking and being self-absorbed and opinionated, it is better to hear the other's point of view and opinion and be present to listen to his feelings with the intention of understanding rather than with the intention of expressing your opinion only. Everyone appreciates a listening ear and a compassionate presence.

15. SAYING "YES" WHEN YOU MEAN "NO."

Being honest about your feelings and expressing them clearly and candidly instead of agreeing all the time helps set clear boundaries in a relationship from the get-go. It indicates that you honor yourself and will not be taken advantage of. Ultimately, your self-respect will remain intact, and you will gain the respect of your partner in return.

16. REFUSING TO COMPROMISE.

To grow your relationship and keep it healthy and loving, it is not important to always be right or to have your way all the time. Life is about compromise. It's about giving and receiving so that each feels cared for.

17. WITHHOLDING LOVE.

Giving the silent treatment to prove your point can be devastating to the emotional health of your relationship. Withholding love to show your disapproval and to punish another for something that does not sit well with you is petty and mean behavior. When something bothers you, it is best to communicate your concern. Oftentimes, you will find that your partner is not even aware of what he may have done, and you were reading so much more into something that may have been an innocent oversight. If you don't air your feelings, how will he know the cause of your angst, and how will he be allowed to make amends? Having an open and calm discussion can alleviate what can easily escalate into a major misunderstanding that may even culminate in a separation.

18. CONSTANTLY TRYING TO PROVE THE OTHER WRONG.

Proving you are right and the other person wrong only brings bitterness to the relationship and does not serve anyone. Ask yourself what is more important: being kind or being right? You don't have to agree to everything another says, but respecting your partner's opinion is a better choice and brings peace into the relationship.

19. REFUSING TO FORGIVE AND ONLY BEING INTERESTED IN GETTING EVEN.

If you have experienced hurt and pain from the actions of your partner, it's best to talk it out. Allowing resentment to fester and lashing out at another cannot heal a relationship. The best of us make mistakes, and sometimes your partner can be careless or is unaware of what he has done. Trying to get even because your partner has hurt you only creates more pain. Forgive and move forward by letting go.

20. SHARING YOUR PROBLEMS WITH OTHERS.

When things go wrong or there are misunderstandings that cannot be resolved, it is best to talk things out in the privacy of your own space. Airing your dirty laundry in public or sharing your problems with family and friends can destroy a relationship, especially as people offer opinions and biased observations without getting the clear picture from both partners.

21. TAKING EVERYTHING PERSONALLY.

   Nothing others do or say is because of you; their vocalizations or actions are just a reflection of themselves and of their own inner turmoil. Allowing your partner to affect you personally can keep you offended for life.

22. BEING PRESENT ONLY WHEN THINGS ARE GOING RIGHT.

   For a relationship to be healthy and long-lasting, each must know that he or she can count on the other to be there through the good and the bad, the happy and sad times, available to give emotional support, provide a listening ear—to hold and lift the other up when it is needed most.

23. EXPECTING YOUR PARTNER TO BAIL YOU OUT OF EVERY DIFFICULTY.

   Each person in a relationship has his or her own challenges. It is not anyone else's job to solve all your difficulties and handle your personal sorrows. But your partner can certainly be there to support you as you handle your pain and to help lift your spirits.

24. BEING SLOPPY IN KEEPING YOUR COMMITMENTS.

   Sloppiness with commitments indicates that you do not cherish each other's feelings. To maintain your respect for each other, make and keep commitments to the best of your ability.

A relationship can only thrive if each makes an effort to make the other happy and appreciated. Couples stay with each other mainly for the emotional and spiritual long-term fulfillment. Men, especially, stay with women they can make happy, and men eventually leave women they can't make happy mentally and emotionally because they feel that they have failed. Ultimately, it's important to share a common foundation of honesty and trust, cooperation and respect, with the understanding that your partner's happiness is equally important as your own. It is part of the incredibly blessed dance in relationships that matter.

"I have lived on the lip
of insanity,
Wanting to know reasons,
Knocking on a door. It opens.
I've been knocking
from the inside."

—Rumi

CHAPTER TWENTY

TWELVE THINGS NEVER TO SETTLE FOR IN A RELATIONSHIP

She came alone into my bridal salon, seemingly very rushed to try on a particular wedding gown and to place her order. I noticed how unhappy and tense she was and convinced her to take a deep breath and spend a little time with me for a brief "consultation." I knew the style she wanted was totally wrong for her slim figure and wished to help her make a better choice.

She agreed, all the while nervously looking at her watch. I could clearly see that she was miserable. Purchasing a bridal gown and planning a wedding is supposed to be fun, I told her. Why was she not enjoying the process? A kind word is all she needed, and she broke down and cried.

This is Caroline's story: The man she was marrying was extremely wealthy and also very demanding. He was the one who had picked out the dress and made sure that she not "waste" her time trying on anything else. This is what he wanted her to wear. He gave her only thirty minutes to purchase the dress and then get back to her house. He had her cell phone and her every move monitored and knew exactly where she was at any given time.

I thought to myself, "This is crazy." The woman could have any man she wanted. She was an accomplished yoga teacher and extremely beautiful, intelligent, and personable. Surely she saw what she was getting herself into?

DON'T SETTLE FOR RESTRICTIVE RELATIONSHIPS

Caroline's story is a classic example of women who settle for relationships that restrict and impair, those who are willing to follow the rules set by their partners and have no voice of their own. They give up their love, their passions, their friendships, and their lives for their partner. They fail to recognize the red flags that so blatantly stare them in the face.

A healthy relationship is supposed to add freedom and life to our existence. It is not meant to diminish us so that someone else can be made to feel better. It's important to own your own power, have healthy beliefs, and speak your truth about yourself and your life to allow soul mate love to become your destiny.

Giving up your identity for someone ultimately chips away at your self-worth and diminishes your self-respect. You are worthy of love exactly for who you are. You don't have to change, to prove yourself, to do anything except be yourself. In being you, you are worthy of tremendous love.

It's so important to remember what you need *never* give up to be in a relationship:

1. **YOUR SENSE OF IDENTITY.**

    Know that you are magnificent already. You may think that you're not good enough, but don't undervalue yourself or what you're capable of becoming. You want to be with someone who appreciates you just as you are, even with your imperfections, because he really sees you instead of wanting to change you.

2. **YOUR RIGHT TO MAKE YOUR OWN DECISIONS IN YOUR OWN TIME.**

   Do what feels right for you and don't give your power away. In relationships, there will be compromises, but even so, you must have the space to think and to do what feels fair. Give, but don't allow yourself to be used. You don't have to settle, and there is no need to rush into any commitment if you're not ready. Don't allow others to control your happiness. Your instincts will guide you, so pay attention.

3. **THE RIGHT TO CHOOSE WHO YOU LET INTO YOUR LIFE.**

   Any relationship that restricts you from seeing other important people in your life, such as your family and friends, and closes you off from the world is not worth pursuing. It's time to break free. This is manipulation, possession, and obsession, and it's a far cry from true love. You are allowing yourself to be robbed of your self-esteem and personal freedom to choose.

4. **THE FREEDOM TO SPEAK YOUR TRUTH.**

   Sharing your thoughts and feelings candidly and with integrity and sincerity makes for a wholesome relationship. Your aim is to be heard and to be understood. Ultimately, it's about being authentic, not giving away your self-respect, being true to yourself, and standing firm in your beliefs.

5. **YOUR BODY IMAGE AND YOUR SELF-ACCEPTANCE.**

   Believing you must change your body image to win another's love does not serve you. Your decision to do whatever you wish must be for you and for your own health and well-being—not for another. It must be your conscious choice for how *you* want to be. There is an unrealistic expectation in society that a woman must be a certain size, must dress a certain way, and must have certain material things to be worthy of attracting love. The media flaunts images of models who are sizes 0, 2, and 4, but in actual fact, 80 percent of women in the world are between sizes 14 and 22. Accept your body as it is, and be comfortable in your own skin. Language is very powerful because it's a declaration of what you believe to be true, so only speak kind words about yourself to yourself. The man who is worthy of you will be one who loves the entire package you're in without wanting to change a thing.

6. **CHEMISTRY, COMPATIBILITY, AND COMMUNICATION.**

    It does not matter how cute or educated and successful your partner is; if you don't feel the kind of sexual attraction that gives you that funny feeling in the pit of your stomach when you are in the same room, then you lack chemistry. Are you compatible as far as your morals and ethics, values and beliefs, religion and politics, educational background, and financial standing? All of these contribute to sustaining a strong bond and friendship. Communication is extremely important. Beyond what you see outwardly, you need to enjoy each other's company and be able to communicate openly and engage in interesting conversations.

7. **YOUR INNER PEACE AND JOY.**

    Never allow anyone to rob you of your joy. You have the freedom to: sing out loud, paint your walls, write poetry, read whatever you fancy until the wee hours of the morning if you wish, love and laugh, sip your favorite wine, play your favorite music and dance, meditate when you want to, do yoga, do whatever it takes to bring inner peace and make you whole. There is nothing worse than coming to the end of life and realizing that you wasted your life living on someone else's terms, always tiptoeing, afraid to laugh, to sing, or to just be silly!

8. **YOUR EXPECTATIONS FOR YOURSELF AND YOUR LIFE.**

   Follow the path that makes most sense for you, and always be true to yourself. Just as everyone has dreams and struggles, you too have yours. Living someone else's idea for your life can result in resentment and misery. Always be yourself and walk your own path. Your life goals matter, so make sure to communicate them clearly and allow your partner to share his as well so that you may support each other toward their fulfillment.

9. **YOUR EXPECTATIONS OF HIS COMMITMENTS.**

   A man who does not live up to the commitments he makes shows he lacks responsibility. In order to build a trusting relationship, your partner must live up to his commitments. Does he do what he says he is going to? Does he show up when he is supposed to, or at least call ahead if he is running late? Or does he make you wait constantly? A man shows his love by the commitments he willingly makes and keeps.

10. **PUTTING UP WITH ADDICTIONS OF ANY KIND.**

    Addiction is anything that takes a person away from handling the normal responsibilities of daily life. There are many kinds of addictions—

drinking, smoking pot, gambling, shopping, computer games, pornography—anything and everything that takes the person away from being present, from being calm or authentic. Addicted people are unable to show up, to handle stuff, to be responsive in a loving way to your needs and requests. They avoid issues that need their attention and live in a world of make-believe. They become overly angry and full of rage if they are deprived or if they are in the throes of their addiction. Their behavior easily and often turns abusive.

There is not much you can do, nothing you can fix. This is their battle, one *they* must wish to overcome and master, and one they must be *committed* to overcoming. You can't change them, and you can only be present and support them from afar, if possible, until they are completely healed. Know that you are powerless over what that person is going to do. Make a commitment to take care of your own self, surround yourself with your own support system, and establish your boundaries. Give them time to prove they are committed to their recovery and allow them to use their time to get their act together. You will know what feels best for you and make your own decision whether to stay or leave.

11. YOUR SELF-RESPECT.

Let's face it, there are some dysfunctional men who love to control and manipulate. They can become very dominant and disrespectful and threaten you if you should go against their wishes. If you don't set your boundaries early on and train your partner to respect you then you're sending the message that he can always expect you to be that way, and he will walk all over you. Maintain your integrity and uphold your self-respect. Assert yourself and instill in your partner a clear sense of respecting your boundaries.

12. CONSTANT SACRIFICE.

In your frustration and desperation, you feel that you must sacrifice for love; you feel like you have to give in constantly to the needs of your partner, to please him, in order to be loved. Soon, you end up having all this built-up anger and resentment because you're running on empty and you realize that you're really not getting what you want from the relationship. You over-give and you do everything to earn his love. You have all the evidence that he can't be the man you want him to be, and yet you stay and give more. You find yourself in the same predicament with everyone you meet because the pattern sneaks in even though you promised yourself that you were going to draw a boundary and take care of your needs first. You have not learned what it is to *receive* love, and until you do, your relationships cannot shift and change.

LET GO OF LIMITING BELIEFS THAT SABOTAGE YOUR CHANCES AT LOVE

Countless women have settled for less because it never occurred to them that they deserved better. Some have only known mediocrity and believe that they are lucky to have found a man who wants to be in a relationship with or perhaps even marry them. He may be someone who criticizes you about a lot of little things or even compares you with his former relationships and lets you know that you will never be able to measure up to his ideal choice. Yet you remain, and you feel lucky to be with the person.

Some have gone through breakups with toxic partners and been drawn right back to them just because they believed this was the best they could do. It is familiar, therefore it must be right. Others have been "ghosted" by men, dumped and ignored often enough that when they meet someone who continues to court them, they immediately gravitate toward them and think this is "love," all the while not really bothering to know their partner's true personality.

Then there are those who are so afraid of being in the same old, same old relationships that they have decided to give up. They don't allow themselves to date and are constantly living their lives on high alert thinking they have to be in control and never trust men again. They are so wounded and afraid of choosing men who aren't capable of stepping up and taking the lead and being the man. They dwell in this limiting belief about being the only one capable of taking care of themselves and find reasons to say no to any man who wants to date them. They yearn to be with someone they can feel really safe with, someone they can relax and be their authentic selves with, but they are afraid to let anyone in.

The key, then, is to start recognizing and then letting go of the beliefs and patterns of behaviors that are limiting you and sabotaging your chances at love. Some, in fact many, of these beliefs stem from early childhood when we believed that we had to do this, that, and the other to please our parents and be loved, or from how we saw our parents or our caretakers behave around us and with each other when we were growing up. It is these limiting beliefs that lead us to think that love must be earned. The truth is, we want to be loved for who we really are; we don't want to have to earn love by constantly *doing, doing, doing* in a relationship.

The fear of not meeting someone more worthy, kind, loving, compassionate, caring, and respectful convinces a woman that she should perhaps settle for the person who is in her life at the moment lest he leave her for someone else. Unfortunately, she believes that putting up with rudeness and inappropriate behavior is better than not having a man in her life at all. Or she mistakes lust for love because of the overwhelming excitement she feels around the person and the obsessive feeling and the uncontrollable urge to be with him. "This must be love," she tells herself.

On the other hand, there are the perfectionists. They will reject a date if there is a typo in his e-mail! It's that mentality where they demand the best of themselves and constantly beat themselves up to do better, to be better, to do more, and they expect the same perfection from others. That mentality limits them and keeps them from having the love that they want and yearn so much for.

Money is another factor that seduces a woman to remain in a relationship. The relationship may be abusive and strip her of her self-worth, but just the fact that she can have a luxurious lifestyle by committing to the relationship is enough for her. Little does she realize that she is clearly being bought, and that a relationship whose foundation is as fickle as this rarely lasts long.

Rather than settling for just anyone, it behooves us to wait until we do meet someone we deserve and who will love and cherish us for the long haul. In the meantime, do everything you can to fill to the brim with love of self; grow that self-worth muscle so that you can be strong enough and intentional in your choice when love does knock on your door.

From that open space of receiving and letting in true love, ask yourself:

- How would I feel?
- How would this union allow me to function in the world?
- What would it feel like to relax and know that I can count on my beloved to be there for me no matter what?
- What would my life be like then?

When you have reached the state of self-awareness and self-love, your feelings and emotions will guide you, and you will recognize true love when it enters your life. And if you find yourself in the old story again, and your emotions get triggered, you will have enough awareness to interrupt that story, move away, and write a new chapter. The choice is yours.

Self-love is the most nurturing kind of love there is. Without self-acceptance, one cannot have self-love. The most important person in your relationship is *you*. Unless you accept yourself and all those parts of yourself, with all the flaws and imperfections, and are true to yourself, you cannot have self-love, and you will always find it challenging to love another.

Have the courage and the willingness to live your life, to love. Fail forward if you must. Life is one huge, big experiment, and you are constantly learning and growing. Be the best *you*. *You matter!*

"If we are not together in the heart, what's the point? When body and soul are not dancing, there is no pleasure in colorful clothing."

—Rumi

CHAPTER TWENTY ONE

NINETEEN RELATIONSHIP MYTHS: EXPECTATIONS VS. REALITY

> "We come to love not by finding
> a perfect person, but
> By learning to see
> an imperfect person perfectly."
>
> —Sam Keen

It seems like you had finally found "The One" only to have him walk away after a few lunches and dinners. You feel like this is déjà vu, and that you are on this perpetual merry-go-round, meeting the most amazing men only to lose them soon after. This can't be happening! You are exhausted and ready to give up because you feel perhaps something is wrong with you and it is not in your stars to be in a happy relationship like so many of your friends and coworkers.

Many of you can relate to this scenario. When one is young and idealistic, one believes they will never meet anyone who is "perfect' for them. Perhaps you have been conditioned from childhood to believe that to have a partner who is strong and powerful, you must be submissive and more "feminine," not so opinionated or strong or powerful. You must constantly listen and tell your man how interesting he is and do everything it takes to elevate his ego so he likes you. So, you end up taking care of the other person and giving much more than you are receiving, only to learn in the end that he really does not appreciate you nor does he respect you.

If you feel that you can never seem to hold on to a relationship despite all your best efforts, then it is time to look at some of the beliefs and expectations you have of your partner. Misplaced expectations in a relationship can be subjective and biased and are merely opinions that do not match up to the other person's thoughts and persona.

MISPLACED MISCONCEPTIONS AND EXPECTATIONS

The biggest misconception we have is that our partner must reciprocate all our feelings and agree with our opinions all the time. It is important to accept the fact that men are wired differently from women and vice versa. The way each of us approaches life situations and challenges is different, and to accept these differences and allow room for understanding the other is key to lasting happiness.

Expectation without appreciation leads to frustration and ultimately conflict in relationships. Some expectations that have no place in any happy and healthy relationship are the following:

1. **I MUST BE THE CENTER OF HIS UNIVERSE.**

    As much as one can wish that were the case, you must understand that each of you had a life, relationships, family, and jobs before merging together. Even though you are very important to each other, each of you still has room to nurture other aspects of your lives. Having a partner who doesn't cling to you, who encourages you to grow, and gives you the freedom to go out into the world knowing that you will come back to him because you love each other is what true love is. It is important that you afford him the same courtesy and understanding so that your love and friendship can grow.

2. **WE MUST AGREE WITH EACH OTHER ALL THE TIME.**

   To expect this means that you each must always live up to the expectations of the other. True success in a relationship is not about having to constantly seek approval and agreement for your own decisions in life but to dare to be yourself and follow your path. Nor should you feel that your partner has to live up to your expectations. The more you approve of yourself, the less you need approval from others.

3. **HE MUST RESPECT ME AS MUCH AS I RESPECT HIM.**

   Love and respect yourself enough that you never have to beg your partner for attention and validation. Having faith and trusting who you are and taking care of yourself shows your partner that you deserve the same from him. When you are happy, when you practice self-love and self-respect, you become a better friend, a better lover, and above all, a better you.

4. **HE MUST NEED ME AS MUCH AS I NEED HIM.**

   Needing someone is like saying that you feel unwanted and unworthy. Value yourself enough that you will never "need" anyone. Conforming to someone else's opinion of how you should be and behave and allowing him to criticize you can destroy your self-worth. When you value yourself, the world values you. Be yourself.

5. THE SUCCESS OF OUR RELATIONSHIP DEPENDS ON HOW GOOD OUR SEX LIFE IS.

Placing overemphasis on the importance of sex above everything else in the relationship has become the main focus and the common belief of today's generation of dating couples. Unfortunately, the physical act of sex alone does not a good relationship make. Granted, sex is important, but basing your relationship only on how good your sex life is will never get you to the blissful connection essential to a long-term, healthy relationship. Willingness to go through the day-to-day process of getting to know yourself through the eyes of another, and growing together, is what true love is all about. Accessing and sharing love with your partner is love.

6. OUR RELATIONSHIP SHOULD BE EASY.

In relationships, as in life, there are always ups and downs, good days and bad days. Good relationships require work, sacrifice, and compromise. How easy your relationship is will depend on how much effort you put into making it so. Reactions to events can determine the outcome. It's all about being there for each other, supporting each other through challenges, especially when it is not so convenient.

7. HE SHOULD CHANGE FOR ME IF HE LOVES ME.

You loved your partner just as he was when you were dating. Expecting someone to change to please you, to distort him to fit your own image, is practically impossible. The image of what you want him to be, and your perception of him, are against the reality of who he truly is. Appreciate your partner just as he is. When you accept and don't try to change people, when you support and allow them to be perfectly themselves, they gradually change right before your eyes. And you will suddenly realize that what has actually changed is the way you now see them.

8. HE SHOULD KNOW WHAT I'M THINKING AND FEELING.

Your partner is not a psychic and may be clueless about what you are thinking at any given point in time. He could be preoccupied with his own thoughts and not realize that you need something. Say what you need to say, share your thoughts, and let him know what you would like and what concerns you. Don't be shy, awkward, or uncomfortable. Express your love. Share your life with him openly and honestly.

9. HE SHOULD SACRIFICE HIS FRIENDS/TIME/FAMILY FOR ME.

Balance in a relationship is important. Just as you need some time away to be whole, he does so as well. Set aside certain days and times where you take a break to spend some time with your friends and family and when he gets to do the same. If you neglect other relationships in your life, your relationships will end up neglecting you, too. Be there for others in your lives as well as for each other. Take time to care.

10. HE WILL ALWAYS MAKE ME HAPPY.

Happiness is our natural state of being, and yet in the natural world we live in, it can be a long way from our current reality. Many things can happen in your daily life to take away your peace of mind, such as problems at work, the weather and traffic, your nosey relatives, or the diving stock market, to name a few. Just as your emotions go through a roller coaster, so can his. Recognizing this truth will help you bring your focus back to your love for each other. Coming from a place of love and understanding and empathy, instead of taking everything personally, will keep you happy.

11. HE WILL TAKE CARE OF ME FINANCIALLY.

Money is one of the most sensitive subjects in a relationship. Unless you have an understanding from the very beginning, this may be quite an unrealistic expectation. Depending on who is earning more income in the household, and what agreement is in place, you should be prepared to share your responsibilities and contribute to the running of your household as well as other needs and wants.

12. OUR LOVE IS ALL WE NEED.

The most powerful relationship you will ever have is the one with yourself. Don't be in love with the mere idea of love, but really and truly love your partner. Your love will go through several tests and challenges. If you can remember to come from a place of love, then and only then can this expectation be fulfilled. Learn to love yourself first rather than looking to your partner to love and validate you.

13. MY RELATIONSHIP WITH HIM WILL SOLVE ALL MY PROBLEMS.

This is the wrong reason to marry anyone. If you feel you have problems, and you're not comfortable enough with your life situation and not "in your own truth" just yet, then you are not ready to be in a relationship. Expecting another to solve all your problems, existing or otherwise, is the direct route to disaster.

14. I MUST BE MEEK, DOCILE, AND CONSTANTLY GIVING TO RECEIVE HIS LOVE.

That men are not attracted to powerful, strong, conscious women who value themselves for their accomplishments and what they do is merely a myth. Men are attracted to women who celebrate their power without having to "play small," those who value themselves for who they are, not what they accomplish. You are extremely attractive when you celebrate the relationship and love in your life over your achievement and success. When you can be authentically vulnerable by sharing your successes and your struggles with your partner, including him in your wins and your losses, you show him how much you value him in your life.

15. I MUST CHANGE MY BODY IMAGE TO BE LOVED.

We measure ourselves, and our self-worth, by society's standards, which are neither true nor realistic. Most women tend to judge their bodies and think they are not good enough to be loved. We have issues like, "If only I could lose twenty, thirty, or forty pounds, he would love me more," "If only I could fix this, I could have the perfect man," and on and on. Our self-esteem takes a nasty dive as we battle our inner critic. The reality is that there is someone out there looking for you in the exact package you're in now. And if you have to change for someone to feel accepted, then he is not the one for you.

16. IF WE LOVE EACH OTHER, WE SHOULD NEVER HAVE TO SAY WE'RE SORRY.

All relationships require constant forgiveness. There will be mistakes and failures, and you will often stumble on your way to learning about each other and sharing your lives. Articulating lovingly, accepting your mistakes, and then apologizing for them means that you are intentional about working on building a strong relationship with your partner. You must also learn to forgive often and quickly, to let it go, and let bygones be bygones.

17. I WILL NEVER BE LONELY BECAUSE I HAVE HIM IN MY LIFE.

Not true. As women, there are times when we feel sad and lonely for no reason. Blame it on hormones! There will be times when you have to be away from each other for travel or other reasons; sometimes, even when you are together and among relatives and friends, you might feel disconnected and alone. It is at such times when you must learn to be comfortable with your own company. Occupy yourself with good books, music, friends, love, and laughter so that you are perfectly fine with being alone and not feeling lonely.

18. HE WILL LOVE MY FAMILY AND FRIENDS BECAUSE HE LOVES ME.

We live in a society where many of us belong to dysfunctional families. Just because he married you does not mean that he has to like your family. Courtesy and politeness will go a long way, but do not expect him to feel the same way about your family that you do.

19. **HE WILL SHARE EQUAL RESPONSIBILITY AND TIME IN RAISING OUR CHILDREN AND MAINTAINING OUR HOUSEHOLD.**

   All things are not created equal. Your job (or his) may require that one of you spend more time raising your children and overlooking and handling your household chores and responsibilities. The subject of who will be responsible for what should be discussed at the onset of your marriage and mutually agreed upon to avoid conflicts and discontentment later on.

Going into your relationship with eyes wide open and a willingness to do whatever it takes to nurture it will multiply your happiness and ensure its success. Above all, hope for the best, expect more from yourself instead of your partner, and you will never be disappointed.

"Whenever we manage to love without Expectations, Calculations, Negotiations We are indeed in heaven."

—*Rumi*

FINAL THOUGHTS

*I*t has been a huge learning curve.

Long-term relationships and marriage are as complicated as we allow them to be. One is a testing ground while the other is a very serious step to take in life. It means: "for better or for worse, in sickness and in health, till death do us part." Or at least you hope so.

A happy and healthy marriage is one of the greatest joys of life, a joy that multiplies manifold when shared with another. You know now what you need to make your relationship strong and durable. Sharing your life with someone else is a commitment that must not be taken lightly. It requires your full-on presence, your complete focus, and your unwavering confidence and cooperation.

Even if you have yet to meet your soul mate, you can start by *believing* that he is already in your life. Believe in *having* the love that you seek, that you deserve it, and that it is already yours. Act *as if*.

In addition to doing the work and becoming clear on your desires, as well as holding on to the vision of what your life would feel like, you can seek help from the Divine by inviting the forces, energy, and intelligence of the Universe to work with you, to be by your side.

You hold the key in your hands. You have the power and the ability to manifest your soul mate into your life. Set out a clear enough request, and have unwavering faith that he is already yours.

The Universe is waiting for you.

Thank you for allowing me to be a part of your journey.

Rani St. Pucchi

"What you seek is seeking you."

—*Rumi*

ABOUT THE AUTHOR

Over thirty years ago, Rani St. Pucchi took the bridal world by storm despite having no formal training in fashion. She is an award-winning couture fashion designer and founder of the world-renowned bridal house St. Pucchi. A passionate and dynamic entrepreneur who launched her global empire in the United States in 1985, Rani's vision was to create an avant-garde bridal and evening couture line with modern styling and classic details. That vision has been realized today.

Famous for infusing her creations with touches of magnificently colored jewels, exquisite hand embroidery, delicate beading, and sparkling crystals on the finest silks and laces, these inspired designs with innovative draping evoke the timeless elegance every woman desires. As one of the foremost designers to introduce exotic silk fabrics and hand embroidery, Rani is applauded for being a pioneer in bringing color to the United States bridal scene, having learned that white does not flatter everyone.

Rani has been recognized and nominated on multiple occasions for her design talent and has won numerous awards as a style innovator. In addition, she has been honored with the Best Bridal Designer Award at the prestigious Chicago Apparel Center's Distinctive Excellence in Bridal Industry (DEBI) Awards.

Rani is famous for designing the wedding dress worn by the character Phoebe on the finale of the hit television show *Friends* as she captured the hearts of millions when she said "I do" in a unique St. Pucchi lilac-colored, corseted-bodice, A-line gown.

Her range of avant-garde designs have been worn by the world's most discerning brides, including celebrities and style icons such as the wife of New York Giants player Aaron Ross, Olympic gold medalist Sanya Richards; Dallas Cowboys quarterback Tony Romo's wife, Candice Crawford; actress Tara Reid; Jason Priestley's wife Naomi Lowde; actress Candice Cameron; and Grammy Award-winning country-music singer Alison Krauss, who donned a specially designed Chantilly-lace-and-silk gown at the Country Music Awards.

Rani has enjoyed much media attention. Her signature designs have been recognized in high profile media such as *Entertainment Tonight, Harper's Bazaar, WWD, Town and Country, Bride's, Cosmopolitan Brides, Inside Weddings, Martha Stewart Weddings,* and *The Knot.*

Having worked with thousands of women, Rani has also become well known for her expertise on how a woman's self-image and self-confidence affect her sense of style and her relationships. Rani is a relationship expert who is on a mission to empower women and make them feel better about themselves so they can make wise choices. Rani believes that confidence must start with a woman's love and acceptance of her body and that when a woman is whole and fulfilled in herself, she makes better relationship choices.

Writing has always been Rani's passion. Since she majored in English literature and poetry, it was inevitable that she would embrace writing and add the role of author to her roster of accomplishments.

In the book *The Soul Mate Checklist*, Rani walks women through their journey of finding true soul mate love. She holds her readers by the hand, guiding them step-by-step in every phase of the path they must navigate before reaching that place of bliss.

In addition to the book you are reading now, Rani is the author of *Your Body, Your Style*: *Simple Tips on Dressing to Flatter Your Body Type*. Renowned for her savvy knowledge of a woman's form and fit, Rani is eager to share her knowledge of more than three decades with all women so they can make better styling choices.

In addition to the book you are reading now Rani is also the author of: *Your Body, Your Style: Simple Tips on Dressing to Flatter Your Body Type* and *Your Bridal Style: Everything You Need to Know to Design the Wedding of Your Dreams.*

Her upcoming books include:

- *Secrets About Success Every Woman Should Know*

- *Unveiled: A Celebrity Fashion Designer's Story: A Memoir of My Life's Journey*

Born and raised in Bangkok, Thailand, Rani now happily lives in Los Angeles, California.

Learn more about Rani at www.ranistpucchi.com

ALSO BY RANI ST. PUCCHI

YOUR BODY, YOUR STYLE:
SIMPLE TIPS ON DRESSING TO FLATTER YOUR BODY TYPE

RANI ST. PUCCHI teaches you simple tricks on how to dress your body in a way that will enhance your best assets and camouflage areas that you feel uncomfortable about or find lacking in any way.

Elevate your self-confidence by defining your personal style and becoming clear on how you wish to be seen in the world.

Learn a simple process to determine what colors flatter you most and which ones to part with so that you may look more interesting, more assured, and in control.

Receive smart shopping tips, learn the importance of investing in the right lingerie, immerse yourself in simple style advice for your body type and more ...

Embrace your unique personality and shine with your body and your style.

YOUR BRIDAL STYLE: EVERYTHING YOU NEED TO KNOW TO DESIGN THE WEDDING OF YOUR DREAMS

Your wedding day is possibly the most important day of your life, and your wedding dress may be the most important garment you will ever wear. Why not take control of the entire process of planning your ideal wedding – one that is fun, intimate and uniquely your own?

In *Your Bridal Style*, award-winning bridal designer Rani St. Pucchi shares her expert advice on everything a bride needs to create a truly unforgettable day, including:

- How to define your personal style based on your specific body type.
- Different wedding silhouettes and what is suitable for different venues and ceremonies.
- A helpful timeline for planning your wedding.
- Do's and don'ts for wedding dress shopping.
- Tips on choosing fabrics, colors, accessories and other finishing touches.
- How to avoid common wedding day mishaps.
- A FAQs section which answers 53 of your most pressing questions.
- Strategies for the photo shoot, and so much more.

This engaging, beautifully illustrated book is a treasure trove of ideas and inspiration. With this book in hand, any bride-to-be can design and create the wedding of her dreams.

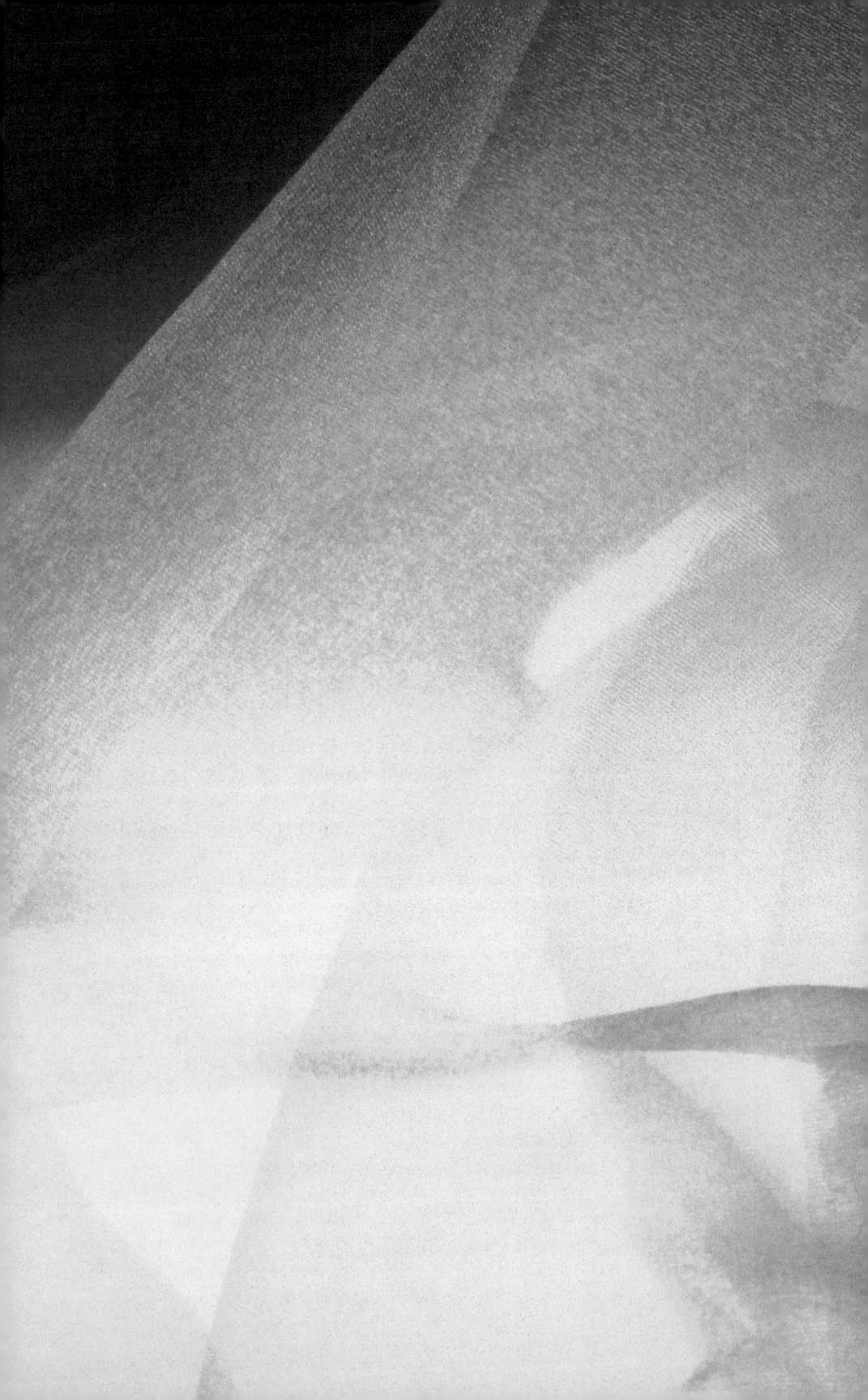

www.ingramcontent.com/pod-product-compliance
Lightning Source LLC
Chambersburg PA
CBHW040333300426
44113CB00021B/2740